THE MYSTERY OF YOU

The
Mystery
of You

FREEDOM IS CLOSER
THAN YOU THINK

Emilio Diez Barroso

LIONCREST
PUBLISHING

Hardcover ISBN: 978-1-5445-2909-7
Paperback ISBN: 978-1-5445-2910-3
Ebook ISBN: 978-1-5445-2911-0

To all my teachers

CONTENTS

INTRODUCTION

IS THIS IT?

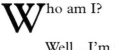ho am I?

Well...I'm me.

Reasonable answer. But did this "me" really appear when I was born, and will it totally disappear when I die? Is that it? Is all of life really about this character doing what it does and then dying? There has to be more to this...

•••

From an early age, I was taught what things were and my place in the world. I started trying on masks and believing what I was told about who I was. I learned to label things and impose a filter on top of my direct experience of reality. My open and curious mind began the process of closing down and subscribing to beliefs and conclusions about everything. What started as a wonder became known as a crayon which then had a utility: to color things with names and to try and stay within the lines. In trying to make sense out of the world, a little of that awe and creativity got replaced by a desire to conform.

Somewhere deep down, however, I knew there was more; I sensed there was a deeper meaning to all of it. What was nudging me, and I believe is calling all of us, is what gives birth to those sporadic existential questions of existence— the kind of questions you ask while looking up at the stars and that, if you're anything like me, you eventually dismiss in order to come back to "reality." Most of us have trained ourselves to turn back from that deep existential inquiry because the enormity and mystery of it can be overwhelming. Somewhere in there, however, there is a part of us that's ready to embark on that adventure, the one that takes us down the rabbit hole that will challenge everything we take for granted. There's another part of us, however, that is very scared. We can call that part the ego. It's not a bad guy; it's simply deeply invested in control and very committed to what's known.

This book is a bit of a roadmap. It's not a roadmap that will give you the answers but rather one that will help you navigate the inner dynamics of both of those parts, the one that is longing for wonder and the one that is coloring inside the lines. The treasure to be discovered in this journey is not a possession but an unraveling of the old ways that awakens our capacity to live from a completely new orientation of being.

This experience of being is not a result of getting the happiness or joy we are taught to pursue as children; it includes that joy and happiness, but it's so much bigger than that. We can stop chasing peace as something to be "achieved" and begin to recognize it as a foundation from which we live. When we are residing in this inner sanctuary, we recognize our OK-ness, even in the middle of the busyness and chaos of daily life, because we're awake to a much larger aperture of existence. The treasure is that we get to live the fullness of who we are because our freedom and well-being are no longer conditioned by external circumstances. Our lives then become an expression of our deepest values. What I am pointing to is not simply a path to become more self-aware, which is fine, but also one that can collapse the entire framework of the egoic identity.

In the chapters that follow, we'll explore how to navigate this from both a psychological and spiritual perspective. These two approaches represent the dynamic balance of who we are and who we are becoming. In other words, we get to grow, heal, and become more self-aware and also gain the recognition that we were never broken. We will examine how our outdated conditioning shows up at the mental, emotional, physical, and spiritual levels and explore a number of valuable tools and techniques that help release the unnecessary baggage that we've been compiling along the way.

•••

Everything you are about to read should be considered descriptive rather than prescriptive. This is an account of the transformation that I've witnessed in myself and others, not a book about scientific facts or metaphysical theories.

The last thing I am trying to do is impose a new set of beliefs on anyone. I simply want to show what's possible and how this unraveling of misunderstandings tends to unfold. I encourage you to approach the journey with your own heartfelt sincerity. Only you can decide and really know what resonates for you and what doesn't. Developing a capacity to discern between resistance and dissonance, something that feels off, allows us to champion our own choices. Ultimately, your greatest compass is a deep commitment to what is true for you.

Most of the self-realization or spiritual books I have read over the years were written by teachers or gurus. I am neither. I have, however, committed a large part of my life to this inner exploration, and I've never been happier. This book is my journey of becoming, bruises and all. I have been inspired to share these experiences with you because those other books were written by authors with lifestyles that didn't match my reality. I wasn't looking to live a monastic life, spending my day silent and in total simplicity. I have children and was involved with all sorts of different business ventures. This caused an internal conflict with competing priorities. On one hand, it felt important to honor my particular life circumstances. On the other hand, I felt a strong pull toward questioning everything and discovering what was true, regardless of the story of my life. I thought that if I wanted to experience that kind of freedom, I was going to have to give up this modern life and live like a monk.

I would get inspired by the possibility of achieving inner peace but then dismiss it as something I could only dedicate myself to once I retired and my kids were all grown up. The life I had was seen as being in the way when in reality it was the way. If you had told me that I could be a board member of over a dozen organizations, running two family offices, managing hundreds of millions of dollars, and parenting three young children while experiencing inner freedom, I would have dismissed it as naïve.

This is my way of normalizing the process of awakening and piercing through some of the erroneous concepts of what enlightenment is. As we get into it, we'll take a deeper look at why we suffer and what's possible when we begin to see an alternative to suffering. We'll look at the various ways in which the ego fights for relevance and explore the tools to liberate ourselves from the mechanisms that keep us imprisoned. As we undo our outdated conditioning and come to the realization of our fundamental wholeness, we will see how we can use our own liberation to fully show up and live our being's greatest expression.

•••

Through my own successes, failures, and encounters with people I have had the privilege of mentoring, the genesis of this book was in the encouragement of those I have supported over the years. I'll share their stories—our stories. I could've written a book about parenting, business, or relationships, but at the core it's really all the same. When we're wearing blue glasses, everything we see is colored. Our conditioning permeates all areas of our lives. How we get triggered in business is likely similar to how we react in relationships or with our kids. Even if the examples don't apply to your life circumstances, I encourage you to consider how they may show up elsewhere. Taking the blue glasses off in one domain of our lives makes it easier to take them off everywhere.

You see, I believe most of us are simply waiting for an invitation. This is my invitation to consider what life could be like outside the paradigm of our fears, doubts, and the societal conditioning we have subscribed ourselves to. Welcome to *The Mystery of You, Freedom is Closer Than You Think.* Let's begin.

○

CHAPTER 1

THE OPERATING SYSTEM

For most of my life, I moved through the world as something of a chameleon. I perfected the ability to adapt to be everybody's ideal: the ideal friend, the ideal business partner, the ideal boyfriend, the ideal son, and so on. I crafted a persona that looked incredibly well put-together, which simply means I had the perfect disguise to hide my insecurities. At the root of them was the fear of not being enough.

I would cope with it by struggling, quite successfully, to appear incredibly secure and self-confident to others. I met and exceeded all the definitions of success that society valued most, but I still couldn't stop comparing myself to everyone around me. It didn't matter what room I was in or what audience I was in front of because I made sure everyone saw me as confident and valuable. I was really good at reading agendas and giving people what they wanted. While some might refer to this personality trait as an asset, it felt like a dysfunction. I felt terribly inauthentic. The truth is, I didn't know who I was.

Our conditioning, what I call the "operating system" human beings run on, was developed over a long period of time. As a species, human beings are around today only because this operating system is able to continuously adapt in order to survive. I'm so grateful for evolution, but our operating system has a bias toward fear, doubt, and worry about… everything. Unlike technology, which develops exponentially, evolutionary updates to our hardware (body) and software (mind) can take many generations. Our life circumstances have shifted dramatically in a relatively short period of time, but our current programming has yet to catch up with our present-day reality.

We continue to react to experiences like rejection in much the same way we did back when acceptance in the tribe was key to survival. If the tribe didn't like you, you risked being cast out and left to die. I knew I wasn't going to die or be killed, and yet I spent so much time and energy trying to control how I was seen by others. I thought if I had something to offer *everyone*, I would be valued and never be alone. The problem was, however, no matter how successful or valued I became to others, I was still chasing recognition. It was exhausting.

One of the main reasons why I invest in a lot of start-up companies is because start-ups are often run by people who question the status quo. They focus on disrupting much larger and more established corporations or industries. To me, that's an exciting arena because the business models and the way we navigate them continue to evolve. In business, it is common to challenge how things are done by searching for ways to optimize or upgrade current assumptions. If this is true for business, why don't we apply the same inquisitive attitude to our daily lives? Is our approach to life working for us, or are we just like these big, established companies, stuck in the comfort of the status quo? Just like them, we're carrying a lot of unnecessary baggage and justify the extra weight by rationalizing and internalizing our dysfunctional behaviors and habits. Like any big business that aims to change how it has been doing things for a while, the comfort of the known needs to be overcome by the recognition of what's possible in the unknown.

The good news is that disrupting these processes and giving ourselves this much-needed upgrade is often easier than we think. We have to start by being willing to take a more active role in determining what continues to serve us and letting go of what doesn't.

ONGOING CONDITIONING

Have you ever heard the story of the married couple who loved to host Thanksgiving dinner for friends and family? The wife was particularly proud of her turkey because she had a unique way of cutting it in half before cooking it. After years of hosting her "split turkey Thanksgiving dinner," her husband finally asked if she really needed to cut the turkey in half before she cooked it. Initially, the wife felt insulted by the question. She said it was an important part of her mother's recipe, but she admitted she really didn't know the reason behind it. Looking for answers, they decided to call her mom to know more about the family secret. Upon hearing the question, her mom quickly burst into laughter. This left the married coupled confused until her mom finally said, "No sweetheart, it's not a family secret. The reason I cut the turkey in half was because, back then, our oven was too small."

How many habits and behaviors did we adopt from our parents and ancestors that are no longer relevant? Sometimes the "devil we know" tricks us into complacency. For a lot of us, the thought of change is overwhelming, even if that change will produce better results. It is impressive how much pain we are capable of enduring before we are willing to challenge the norm. Dictators rely on this type of fear in order to remain in power. They attempt to get away with as much as possible without pushing their people to a breaking point.

Much in the same way a dictator wields fear to control the masses, our ego uses fear, doubt and worry to keep us psychologically imprisoned. It then leverages the promise of a better future in order to keep us from going over the edge and rebelling. This is why some people experience personal transformation when they hit rock bottom. They are finally prepared to lose everything, even their lives, for the possibility of something different.

Why do we put up with all the mental trickery? Why are we so scared to challenge the inner workings of our psychological makeup that we put ourselves through so much hell? We have defaulted to taking our personal dysfunction as a given and strive to cope with things like stress, anxiety, burnout, and depression through all sorts of unsustainable means. We think the only way to overcome the struggle is by suppressing or outrunning it. Instead of examining the internal cause, we attribute the suffering to what's happening "out there." We are convinced when things turn out how we want, all the tension will somehow fade away. We have it reversed. The transformation needs to come from addressing our inner turmoil. By mending the internal, the external has a natural way of realigning itself.

If we could change ourselves, the tendencies in the world would also change. As a man changes his own nature, so does the attitude of the world change towards him...
—MAHATMA GANDHI

THE PURSUIT

Growing up in the eighties, Pac-Man was my game. I could spend hours with a pocket full of quarters. As long as I was winning, life outside of the arcade faded off into oblivion. Sometimes I would be so into it, I wouldn't notice the blisters on my hands until I pried them away from the sweaty joystick. The game is about accumulating points by gobbling more and more things and running away from ghosts. There is no stopping; you just have to keep going, or you die. Sound familiar?

Just like Pac-Man, I was also programmed to value *more*, as are, I think, most of us: more resources, more love, more wealth, more recognition, and so on. Society runs on it, and through the advent of social media, we've even found a way to measure how "liked" we are. We've subscribed to the notion that if we can somehow just get enough of whatever it is that we value, everything will be OK. And look, there is nothing wrong with wanting more, but when our wanting is based on lack and limitation, our core orientation to life becomes one of not enough. "Life is not enough; I am not enough; you are not enough," and so on.

The problem with this orientation is that we live in constant pursuit and our existence becomes entirely focused on the next gobble. This trance of accumulation has us believing that something will somehow fill the vacuum, but nothing does, so we keep going.

When I first contemplated this premise, it didn't quite resonate. I didn't become an entrepreneur because I didn't feel like I was enough or didn't have enough recognition, love, or even money. I became an entrepreneur because I loved the challenge of building things from the ground up and, yes, the process of making money. Later on, I came to realize the distinction between the creative drive and the unrelenting chatter of "more" that produces the inherent anxiety and stress. Whenever I paid close enough attention, I was able to differentiate between the times I was involved with something for the thrill of it and when I was operating from a place of lack.

Over the years, I have had the privilege of starting dozens of companies. It's an exciting adventure and something I still enjoy to this day. The reality, however, is that a lot of these ventures have failed. Sure, it would fit nicely into this paragraph for me to say the businesses where I was purely involved for the thrill of the adventure or the passion projects were the financially successful ones, but it was not that correlated. What I can say for certain, however, is these projects were the ones I enjoyed the most. The main difference between them and the others was the degree of attachment to any particular result. When we operate from scarcity, we become myopic in our vision of desired results. This makes us rigid and susceptible to stress and anxiety. However, when we operate from a place of abundance, or in this case the impulse to create something from nothing, we are ultimately more fulfilled.

All this can be traced back to the conditioning we experienced growing up. As children, filled with lofty dreams and grand possibilities, we may have enjoyed playing sports, painting, or dancing. Then someone, often our parents, gives us praise for how we play, paint, or dance. In a conditioned response, we begin to innocently outsource our self-worth to this form of external validation. We then crave this acknowledgment and start tailoring our behavior in order to obtain it, again and again. This setup has become part of the human condition, because when we receive recognition for our accomplishments, the brain begins to release serotonin and dopamine, also known as the body's feel-good chemicals. Not only do we crave this feeling, but we become somehow addicted to it.

The addiction creates a problem because we now associate the attention, the love, and all the acceptance with our sense of self and belonging. This puts us on a never-ending hamster wheel, chasing validation in every aspect of our lives: family, work, and play. When we don't receive it, we make it mean something about us. The stakes are raised, and a little more attachment is introduced the next time we play, paint, or dance. This dysfunctional scenario is quite present in our schooling. Teachers praise students and parents reward their children when they do well on exams or presentations. The person we are becoming is less important than our accolades and capacity to meet the expectations of others. Curiosity and the love of learning are replaced by the drive to perform and get good grades.

When I was ten years old, I loved writing short stories. Whenever I got positive feedback from family and friends, the attention made me feel wonderful. At one point, I remember feeling the pressure to write an even better story, but I wasn't hearing a new story to tell. I would sit down and *want* to write, but nothing was coming through. Before feeling the thirst for validation, I would write because I loved to; now, it felt different.

Because I wanted to feel the "high" of recognition again, and because I didn't have a story to share, I decided to copy one from a book. I put my name on the title page and passed it off as something I had written. The result was everything I had imagined. People loved it. Friends. Family. Everyone who read it was impressed at how far I had come as a young writer. Well…almost everyone. Sensing I had plagiarized the story, my nanny, who had lived with us since I was three years old and had a way of seeing through everyone in my family, quickly called me out. Knowing something was off, she asked me the meaning of a particular word in "my" story because it was a word way beyond my years. Since I didn't know the meaning of the word I had stolen, I quickly became defensive and shut down. I still remember the word, *ventarrón*, or "gale" in English, and I don't think I've heard the word since. The truth was, I was caught red-handed, and the whole experience was crushing. I was so ashamed of myself. I never wrote again…until now. Talk about taking some time off. To think about the shame and regret I carried because of this experience makes me feel for my ten-year-old self.

This self-induced pressure to be recognized, to be seen in a certain light, ultimately hampered my natural impulse to express myself creatively. Anything that could be judged subjectively, like writing, dancing, or art, felt risky. For most of my life, I could no longer distinguish which preferences or inclinations were authentic and which were encumbered by the expectations I put on myself to manage how I was perceived. Did I really like the world of finance, or was it because I was always good at numbers and liked the attention it got me?

THE MYTH OF ENOUGH

Wouldn't it be great if we could finally get something that would permanently make us feel totally complete? The truth, which we rarely recognize, is that nothing has ever given us a sense of lasting fulfillment or satisfaction. None of the recognition, love, and appreciation we have gotten has or ever will be enough; if it had, we wouldn't still be chasing it. The same goes for the accumulation of possessions, experiences, or achievements; it's like we are attempting to fill a bucket, but it's riddled with holes. We rush to maintain the level and put more water in instead of tending to the underlying cause of the leaking.

I can still remember the feeling I would get when I saw all the presents under the tree on Christmas morning. Every year, I was convinced that getting that one special toy would satisfy me forever. Obviously, that toy never came—a toy like that doesn't exist. And even though I understand this now, that doesn't mean I would ever deny my own children the joy and excitement of opening presents on Christmas morning. It's still fascinating to witness how much anticipation there is for that one thing they so desire, and how quickly the excitement fades a few hours later.

As we grow older, it feels like we have a way of holding on to the same urgings we had as children. We are stuck in a constant loop of searching for the next new something, getting excited when we get it, and then quickly moving on. There's no question that it's fun to play, have toys, and go on fabulous vacations, but consumerism and the pursuit of accumulation has become a socially accepted drug. Like any other form of addiction, we simply justify or deny it as we search for our next high.

This never-ending drive is so engrained, it even applies to those of us who have snapped away from the gravitational pull of the material race. Years ago, I began to reprioritize my life and adopt a whole different set of values. I shifted from being materially motivated to only caring for things that "really mattered" to my heart. At first, it felt like I had broken free from the paradigm of "more," but I hadn't really escaped anything. The energy of "not enoughness" had merely shifted focus. I quickly discovered my attention was still centered on wanting more: more amazing experiences, more balance in life, more knowledge, more meaningful relationships, more impact, more time with the kids, more spiritual insights, and so on. Remember, our programming doesn't like to be still, as it's trained to be constantly on the move.

Choosing to have additional quality time with my children and more balance in work and relationships is certainly valuable and more sustainable than accumulating possessions, but I still hadn't unraveled the underlying operating principle of it all. I was still functioning from the same core premise of not-quite-enough, which keeps our focus on the future and what could be instead of *what is*. Our society has somehow normalized this way of being. It indoctrinates us into the busyness of always being busy by placing our attention on what's coming next. It's one of those recipes passed from generation to generation that needs to be examined.

When we postpone our well-being with ideals like, "When this happens or that happens, then things will be OK," we opt out of being in the moment and opt into a habit of waiting. By hanging out in memory (the past) and imagination (the future), we are missing out on what is happening *right now*. Fortunately, our life hasn't gone anywhere; it's always right here, and there's a way to claim it back.

GETTING HERE

I have never studied Buddhism, but I have always felt a strong connection to the practice. Siddhartha Gautama, the Buddha, was born into a royal family and yet developed a sense of dissatisfaction with his life. This motivated him to leave the comforts of privilege and begin a spiritual quest. In some ways, this is how I felt growing up. My life seemed great, I couldn't really complain, and yet there was an underlying discontentment that led me to ask some of life's big questions.

In Buddhism, the Four Noble Truths are considered among the most important teachings of the Buddha. They are as follows:

- **DUKKHA** (dissatisfaction). Suffering exists and is an intrinsic characteristic of existence.

- **SAMUDAYA** (origin). There is a cause of suffering.

- **NIRODHA** (cessation). There is a way to end suffering.

- **MAGGA** (path). The means to end suffering.

The first Noble Truth is based on an acknowledgment of suffering. It points to discontent, a sense of inadequacy that often resides just under the surface of our awareness. We may not be completely familiar with this dissatisfaction, as we tend to spend a lot of energy trying to avoid feeling it, but it's there. Slowing down enough to acknowledge it can be tough, and sometimes overwhelming, but the truth of suffering is only the first Noble Truth.

Samudaya, the second Noble Truth, states that suffering actually has a cause. It comes from our tendency to grasp at what we don't have, didn't get, thought we deserved—essentially, the insatiable desire for more we've been talking about. When my daughter was around six years old, she asked me what poverty meant. Not your typical question from a six-year-old, I know, but she is not a typical kid. I could have given her the standard definition of poverty and then taught her how fortunate we are, but I had a feeling this would be a cop-out. It didn't represent what I have witnessed in life. So, as she stared at me with her beautiful brown eyes, I said, "Poverty is wanting what you don't have." She seemed to take a minute to unwrap what I had said, then looked up and said, "Like when you wanted Mommy to understand you?" Exactly!

We all know people who have a lot of money and people who don't. There will always be the haves and the have-nots. Money certainly alleviates some of the day-to-day burdens or stress when the bills are due, but it doesn't make us less poor. Haven't we all encountered people who are financially secure but emotionally bankrupt? Know anyone who barely has enough to eat but still seems incredibly wealthy? A person can feel rich or poor at any given moment, because fulfillment is completely unrelated to their purchasing power. There was a period of time in my life when I added the disclaimer, "After having certain needs covered, of course." This was my way of avoiding the uncomfortable commentary of "yes, but you've never experienced living in the streets with your kids." While this might be true, I have come across people who are living in absolute deprivation and still embody a deep sense of inner peace. Moments like this have been a good reminder and realization that freedom is an "inside" job.

The third Noble Truth is Nirodha, which states liberation is possible and that there is an end to suffering. In essence, it is indeed feasible to unravel and become free of the dissatisfaction which has become prevalent in our lives. For most of my life, I convinced myself this kind of freedom was only possible for enlightened masters who lived in the Himalayas or were part of a monastery somewhere. If I wanted that kind of liberation, I thought I was going to have to be like the Buddha and leave my life as I knew it.

The fourth Noble Truth, Magga, shows us there is a path to end the suffering, a way out. Deep down, I believe we are all interested in peace. From the ardent capitalist, who receives it from feeling a sense of accomplishment, to the longtime meditator, who receives it through stillness, we all imagine if things turn out OK, we will finally be at peace. While suffering involves searching for the "next thing," true liberation requires a new approach, one that recognizes our well-being is not going to be found somewhere in the future, because the future is always somewhere else. Whatever we're looking for can only happen in the moment, so we must find a way to get back here.

I wish it were as simple as just acknowledging all experience can only happen right now; then there wouldn't be a need for a path. There would be nowhere to go and the notion of doing something so that we get back to now would be silly. Unfortunately, the habit of being somewhere else runs very deep, so shifting out of it seems to require some active participation on our part. The fourth Noble Truth points the way.

CHAPTER 2

IRRATIONAL DISCONTENT

I was raised in an extremely privileged environment that prized the accumulation of power and money. From an early age, I bought into the common belief that more money and more power would mean more happiness. My somewhat unusual experience was that my family already had far more power and money than we could ever possibly need. Why was everyone around me still trying to get somewhere, and where was this happiness that was supposed to come with wealth? All the external possessions couldn't ultimately mask the fact that I was emotionally impoverished.

On the surface, I certainly lacked for nothing and had no reason to complain. In fact, complaining would have been seen as self-centered and inconsiderate. What's worse, it would also have revealed that I was not as perfect as I appeared. I was a victim of my own need to hide my imperfections. This inner chasm informed most of my actions and kept me striving for perfection everywhere in my life. I didn't want good grades; I wanted the best grades. I didn't just want to be popular, I wanted to be president of the class, homecoming king, most successful businessman, etc.

I never actually acknowledged the inner lack I was feeling in the midst of all the outer abundance. Those feelings were immediately covered and my deep insecurities were hidden, even from me. I focused on receiving as much external validation as possible. Obviously, this was an unsustainable approach.

My father constantly, and no doubt sincerely, insisted that his ultimate interest was my well-being. Nevertheless, I was entirely dependent on gaining and keeping his approval. Growing up, many of my choices were filtered through the lens of how he would perceive them. His authoritarian nature, both as a parent and business leader, modeled for me the stereotype of a successful man. In order to make it, I thought I had to be the same way, but I wasn't. For a long time, I thought I had to choose between honoring my gentler way and succeeding in business.

I was driven and committed to carving out my own path and outrunning the big shadow of my family's success. Because a lot had been given to me, I expected a lot of myself. I was determined to make my mark, and it had to be a big one because my family set the bar pretty high. I wanted to do something and be great at whatever that something was.

Instead of being inspired when my peers were successful, I became competitive. Other people's successes felt threatening to my sense of self. My inner voice was a constant companion. In often subversive ways, it told me, "Look at them, they are already successful, and they started with less than you. You have to be the best and demonstrate value all the time. If you're not, you will fall behind. You'll waste your life. If you stop being admired or having something other people want, you'll become disposable." I am amazed that I could keep functioning. It's like I was trying to maintain my head above water, swimming for survival. It was not only ineffective, it was draining.

SPIRITUAL CARROT

I was raised Roman Catholic and loved how church made me feel. At one point, I even considered the idea of becoming a priest. This apparently noble sentiment was ultimately fueled by my search for personal meaning and value. I was called to something deeper than myself, but because I was so driven and goal oriented, I didn't want to be an ordinary priest. I would be the most special priest of all. If I went into the clergy, I would become pope! It sounds silly, but that's how I approached everything. Even though I wasn't conscious of it then, my interest in religion was an early way of answering a call that eventually pulled me well beyond my comfort zone in order to search for something grander and truer.

I eventually became disenchanted with Catholicism and began pursuing a different direction spiritually. By this time, I had begun to question the idea that more business success was going to somehow make me feel enough. As if sensing its existence was in jeopardy, my ego quickly found something new to go after. If I wasn't going to be either the pope or the most successful and wealthiest businessman ever, I would become the most enlightened person on the planet. My egoic drive found a new channel within the practice of spirituality. This became the ultimate accomplishment. I thought if I became enlightened, everyone would then admire me. I would be extra, extra special and wouldn't have to deal with any of my persistent insecurities. I had found a new, even more sophisticated coping mechanism, and it became my new drug. Little did I know, however, the nature of the journey I had embarked upon was eventually going to unravel all my coping mechanisms and bring up all the underlying issues I had been so invested in avoiding.

I approached spirituality like I approached business—through accumulation. Instead of dollars, I was now accumulating experiences and insights, climbing higher and higher on the ladder of spiritual consciousness. I got a master's in spiritual psychology and read a whole lot of books. I listened to teachers and attended dozens of silent meditation retreats. My drive was now oriented toward this newfound magic pill, spiritual enlightenment.

The work was transformational and life became somehow lighter and even easier to deal with. I became less judgmental and experienced more freedom, which were wonderful improvements psychologically. However, I was developing and becoming attached to a new identity. I felt people should want to be friends with me and love me because I was spiritual—*very* spiritual, whatever that meant. It was a great place for the ego to set up shop, which it did. When we grow attached to our identities, we feel the need to defend them and will resist anything that threatens them. This defensiveness tends to be a good sign that our ego is back in the driver's seat.

PARENTING AS A PATH

There's nothing like children to poke at any egoic construct; they keep me grounded and practical. Parenting has tested, compromised, and essentially destroyed the "enlightened" sense of self I was looking to experience when I chose to follow a spiritual path. It has forced me to face and experience all the disenfranchised parts of myself I had temporarily managed to bypass or bury away deep inside. Being forced to develop this capacity to meet all those parts transformed me, not into a perfect parent, but someone who can at least pass through, if not always be at perfect peace with, the storms that parenting will inevitably bring.

For example, my son is an extremely outspoken boy. From the time he was little, his strong will would often trigger me, push me, and sometimes even enrage me. I didn't want to deal with this because the challenge arrived during a point in my life when my "spiritual identity" was reaching its peak. Or so I thought. I was completely invested in coming across as this peaceful, inspiring, and amazing guy who would never lose his cool. My son had the ability to shatter the idea in the blink of an eye. So, to that, I thank him and say, "Way to go, little man." Teachers arrive in our lives at the moment we need them most. In this case, my teacher was my son. A six-year-old.

Adults have a way of thinking that we have it all together. In my case, I thought, "Father knows best." I don't think it's a stretch of the imagination to say that some of the most spiritual beings on the planet are our children. They are teachers the minute they arrive. They are clear mirrors that will reflect back anything that is unsettled within us. We think we are raising our children, but really, they are raising us, leading us back to an original innocence. I've learned more about myself from being a parent than any spiritual or silent meditation retreat I have ever been on. It's the ultimate retreat, because it doesn't stop when the meditation bell goes off.

Prior to being a parent, it was easier to distance myself and turn to all sorts of coping mechanisms when a relationship became challenging. I would defend my point of view and innocence at any cost. Blaming others was one of my preferred "go-to" strategies. As a parent, this wasn't an option because being a father wasn't something I was willing or able to turn away from. Not that I didn't try to blame my children for my upsets, but I quickly realized the silliness of that approach. No, I knew I would have to take 100 percent responsibility for anything that triggered me. For the first time in my life, I had to face all my "stuff" head on. I was all in, at times quite reluctantly.

CLEAR REFLECTIONS

My experience of the world is that it mirrors how I experience myself. Have you ever noticed when you're having a crappy day that everything seems to turn out crappy?

It's like they say, when it rains, it pours. And for some odd reason, consciously or unconsciously, the misery of it all becomes our chosen company. In reality, the world hasn't actually changed, we are simply perceiving it a certain way, which ultimately reflects our inner state of being moment by moment. What I think about life and about others is more a reflection of me than of the "other."

When we allow people to get close, the way they reflect things back to us is magnified. This is challenging because it forces us to look at things we haven't wanted to or weren't willing to face in our past. We may find it easier to move on, change partners, or stop communicating altogether than face the issues at hand. When you have children, it's harder to run from the responsibility and turn our backs. I think that's part of the reason parents become unavailable, distracted, or spend long hours at work. Being a parent is one of the toughest jobs there is. But we don't need to have children in order to recognize that we can't outrun these dark corners of ourselves forever. Life has a glorious way of presenting situations that poke at our wounds until we are ready and willing to address them. Proof of this is living on the other side of the statement, "Why does this keep happening to me?"

How often have we said to ourselves or heard someone else say something like, "My last five girlfriends have all been the same. Why can't I find someone normal? Why do I end up with business partners who screw me over behind my back?" I believe this is life's little way of orchestrating the redemptive moment when we finally recognize the common denominator in all of these experiences is ourselves. If we want true freedom, we need to shift out of the victim mentality and put our dysfunction on the witness stand. If we continue to "plead the Fifth," we will continue to live imprisoned by our own coping mechanisms and never take responsibility for our lives. I know this is a big ask. I have been there, but I was done with giving away my power. Sometimes all it takes is a willingness to stop trying to be right.

Intimate relationships give us an opportunity to surface, look at, and ultimately embrace all the marginalized parts of ourselves. These parts often remain at the age when the original pain occurred and still relate to what's happening in that way. I have certainly had my fair share of upsets where my reactions resembled those of my eight-year-old self. These reactions can be seen as an invitation to bring awareness into all those aspects of ourselves we have turned our backs on. It's like shining a flashlight on the places in a basement you find a way to avoid cleaning. It's stinky and dark and there are a hundred reasons why we really don't want to go there and clean because it's uncomfortable. At some point, however, we muster the courage and realize that, as bad as it may feel, it is easier to address and clean these places than to keep ignoring them.

When we do, we discover that these unresolved areas within us are just like old wounds. We were never taught to treat them, so we learned to cover them up. Some of them may have been small scrapes and others big gashes; the degree of ongoing pain, however, has less to do with the intensity of the incident and more to do with the conclusions we made about it. An innocent misunderstanding, such as, "There's something wrong with me," can have lifelong implications in how we move through life. That's a hard thing to feel, particularly when we're young, so we employ all sorts of strategies to avoid anything that brings it back up. That's why when something does indeed irritate the wound, we react so poorly and often so disproportionately. Like an infected cut, the healing can only happen if we peel away at some of those protective layers we've created over it.

Encountering these parts with the love and care they didn't get originally is the balm that restores them. This can be as straightforward as visiting the memory of our younger selves with a broader perspective and a restorative attitude. For example, in the situation where I plagiarized as a ten-year-old boy, I went back to that event in my mind and spent time recalling and noticing what was happening, à la the Ghost of Christmas Past. At that time, I felt shame and embarrassment. I somehow concluded that I wasn't creative; therefore, anything that included putting myself out there, like writing, was unsafe. I continued the process of spending time with my younger self and met him with the self-acceptance that I couldn't give myself at that age. I reminded him how much he actually enjoyed writing and that what he had done was a one-off and an innocent mistake. I went as far as to visualize myself as an adult hugging this ten-year-old "me" and telling him I loved him. It was enormously healing.

I had left that assumption unexamined and denied my creativity for a very long time. I didn't go back to try and rewrite history, deny, or justify what happened, I simply examined and updated the assumptions that were created in the first place. By unraveling misunderstandings that perpetuate our discontent, like this one, we can transform the way we relate to the world. Most of us are walking around with a lot of these little wounds. We don't have to go looking for them, as we can always count on life to let us know where they are. Even though parenting was a big catalyst for my introspection, anyone can take the inner journey and clean their house, so to speak.

CHAPTER 3

UNNECESSARY ROUGHNESS

Being human is a crazy ride. We experience love, loss, and have fragile bodies that get hurt and become sick. Yet there is a difference between pain and suffering. Pain happens in the moment and seems to be an inevitable part of being alive. Suffering, however, is optional. If a baby boy falls down, he will cry because falling hurts. Before he's developed a defined sense of self, he doesn't judge his clumsiness or look for someone to blame. All he knows is the pain from falling down. He hasn't formed the additional layer of interpretation about what's happening and doesn't have any sort of opinion about his falling down. Without the commentary about the situation, all he feels is the sensation of pain.

PUSH-PULL

Suffering, at its core, is fueled by consciously or unconsciously trying to have positive experiences and avoid negative ones. It makes perfect sense to desire pleasant situations and experiences over unpleasant ones. The problem, however, is rather than simply having a preference about what we favor, we act as if our preferences were vitally important to our survival. The attachment we place on desired outcomes and the resistance to the ones we want to avoid turn us into micromanagers of our lives. We become narrowly focused on a specific future and forego our ability to remain present because we're busy making sure everything goes according to plan. This energy justifies its existence with the belief that its oversight is required for things to work out. It sells us on the idea that without it, life would somehow fall apart. But life is fluid and everything is in constant change. Forcing things to unfold according to our plans is simply the ego's way of believing it's in control.

It's humbling to accept that we don't know what's best. We think we're going somewhere, and life throws a curveball. What may be perceived at first as a detour ends up being exactly what we needed. Despite how often I was shown this, I was still operating under an "I know better" mentality. I was confident I knew what should happen and found myself stuck in a loop of "must get there," like a little hamster running on a wheel trying to catch the cheese. Wanting to get over there, wherever that is, is essentially saying "no" to this moment. "Right now is not OK, and therefore I'm not OK, so something must change." I'm not suggesting that we stop looking at what could be improved in the world or in ourselves. Learning from our past and modifying our behavior are essential components of being alive, but we are less efficient at creating change when we are in inner turmoil and at war with the moment.

When we realize we are suffering, the logical impulse is to want things to be different. However, this only perpetuates the cycle of suffering because it stems from the same notion of "something is wrong with right now, so I must get to 'then.'" That's the confusion that got us here in the first place. We have learned to delay our well-being and resist what is actually happening by thinking this resistance is necessary for things to change for the better. It isn't. When we are suffering, it's valuable to give ourselves a reality "gut" check. It involves simply asking ourselves, "What is really going on here? What experience am I trying to avoid?" It is important to get still and really curious, because the ego doesn't thrive in a state of presence. It will attempt to throw us back into a loop of suffering by resisting what's happening. Having a reference point may be helpful, so I thought I would model it with stories of people I've known and mentored over the years.

RICHARD

On the surface, my friend Richard's life looked amazing. He had a great job, a great partner, and a wonderful family. His friends loved him, and he had every reason to be happy. The problem, however, was that Richard wasn't happy... at all. The feeling was further complicated by all the guilt wrapped around his unhappiness. He once told me, "I know I should be grateful for everything, but something seems to be missing." We often avoid being vulnerable, but acknowledging what is true for us is much more empowering than pretending something is not there. This first step in addressing an issue is recognizing there is one.

Focusing simply on getting Richard to feel more motivated or happier would be a nice Band-Aid to the situation. I'm much more in favor of looking at the underlying programming that is causing our issue, though, because otherwise it'll keep resurfacing in other ways. In order to reveal what's really going on, we must slow down long enough to become aware of the mechanisms at play. We come to this awareness through introspection, the reality "gut" check I was speaking of earlier. What am I actually feeling? What am I trying to make sure doesn't happen? Questions like these can point us to the root of our resistance.

As a child, Richard had a financially unstable upbringing. Money wasn't always available, and he witnessed the toll it took on his family. His father had made money, but then he lost most of it. He went from being able to afford things to not being able to meet some of his family's basic needs. As an adult, Richard was committed to doing whatever he needed in life so he and his children wouldn't have to experience the same uncertainty.

Early on, Richard chose a path of safety. He secured a middle-of-the-road corporate career because of the stability it provided. And while there is nothing wrong with this path, Richard always felt like he had more to give. He reached a good position in the company but began to notice his growth felt stagnated. He thought he deserved a promotion, but it never came. He even considered joining a startup so he could address the longing to feel more challenged, but that didn't happen either.

When he and I explored what was going on, we discovered there were two opposing forces at work: his desire to grow and be creative, and his fear of losing everything. Even though he desired to step outside of his comfort zone and was excited by the idea of a nimble startup, the underlying worry of making a misstep held him back. In his current job, there were often opportunities for him to take on more responsibilities, but this meant giving up the safety that made him feel at ease.

It was powerful for him to realize that this push-pull dynamic, based on his father's journey, was sabotaging his growth by keeping him "sheltered." At the expense of his own happiness, he was choosing the reliability and safety of his corporate job so he wouldn't go broke. The financial security that was meant to make him feel free had actually become the ball and chain of his discontent. Richard thought that when he had saved enough money, he would finally take the entrepreneurial plunge one day. Without working through the underlying mechanism, odds are that this "one day" would never come, though.

Becoming aware of our behavior can sometimes be enough, but, in my experience, more often than not, we need to implement some practical changes in order to break our unconscious patterns. Richard decided to do one thing a week that felt risky and in the direction of his intention to grow and be challenged. He was going to start by asking his boss what it would take for him to get a promotion. This may seem simple, but it was a huge step for him. What may seem easy for some can be extremely challenging for others. The courage paid off and he started embracing more responsibilities at his job, but, more importantly, there was a new sense of aliveness in him. His programming was no longer unconsciously running him, and he claimed back dominion over his life.

INSOURCING

Whenever I felt my own sense of discontent, I immediately looked for my next "fix." I was in a constant search for something to look forward to. My well-being was dependent on the "something wonderful" that was going to happen... in the future. There is nothing wrong with having anticipatory thoughts or sensations, but I was living out of them. When something didn't happen, or even a short while after that something did happen, I noticed I would experience a subtle sense of depression. Because this dissatisfaction was so uncomfortable, I would quickly rush to find the next thing to feel excited about.

This is so socially acceptable that it has become our standard modus operandi. We have been conditioned to pursue a state of happiness that depends on external circumstances we don't and can't control. "My partner makes me happy. Closing a lucrative business deal makes me happy. Eating this delicious piece of cake makes me happy." These are all ways we outsource the sense of well-being we were originally born with.

This outdated programming can impact so much of our lives, including the way we approach careers. How often have we been told or said to ourselves, "Make sure you're doing something that you love to do." We also hear, "Do what you love, and you'll never work a day in your life." All this sounds sensible and can certainly be inspiring, but it's a double-edged sword. No matter how much you love what you do, the nature of things is that there will be harder days than others. If we do what we do expecting it to bring us joy, what happens when we don't experience that love? Do we then think something's wrong with our job, or do we think something is wrong with us?

We have become conditioned to think that we *need* to find that one job that we love so much that it just naturally makes us happy. We have mistakenly believed something out there, outside of ourselves, will bring about a sense of fulfillment. My actual experience is whatever I'm doing becomes a reflection for what is going on in my inner world. The specifics of what we commit our time to are not as relevant to our happiness as we believe.

According to Dr. Sonja Lyubomirsky, Vice Chair of Psychology at the University of California, Riverside, only 10 percent of our happiness is attributed to circumstances. That means the other 90 percent has nothing to do with what's actually going on. If we don't deal with this core misunderstanding, at some point, no matter how much we enjoy what we do, we will eventually become dissatisfied. We may then come up with a "story" that our job isn't what it used to be—or worse, that something's wrong with us because we no longer enjoy what we used to. Enter the thinking of a midlife crisis.

The word "purpose" is another one of those tricky notions. Since I grew up with what I considered to be tremendous privilege, I felt if I wasn't fulfilling my purpose, I was being wasteful and irresponsible. What I really wanted was to feel important and know that my life mattered and had a special meaning. Every time I felt like my purpose wasn't clear, I would stress out and doubt everything I was involved with. When I talk to people about the word "purpose," I realize my experience wasn't unique. Some of the questions that come up for them are: "How do I find it? I should know what it is by now. This or that person has already found their purpose, so why can't I find mine? I thought I knew what my purpose was, but now, I'm not sure."

The underlying belief is that there is a unique purpose "out there" somewhere that will make our existence worthwhile. If you're not doing that, you are wasting your life. What you do needs to have a specific external effect, and that effect or result will determine your value. When we feel incomplete, we look for completion anywhere we can. We believe if we find our purpose, that void will be filled, and our life will be meaningful. This is simply another way we outsource our well-being.

I often encourage people to think of purpose in terms of "how" and let the "what" follow. I invite them to examine how they want to show up in the world at any given moment. Aside from your actions and their external effects, what does "living with purpose" mean to you? What are the inner characteristics or feelings you experience when you believe you are fulfilling your purpose? By connecting with these qualities, you can "insource" your sense of value and take ownership for how you show up, both in the world and for yourself. You can experience that resolve and purposeful-ness directly, without conditions or intermediaries. When we operate from our core values, we come into alignment with our being's unique expression independently of the work we do or what the results might be.

I am involved with many businesses and nonprofits that are focused on changing the lives of billions of people. I wouldn't be doing it if I didn't think the effort was worth-while. However, I also believe that no matter how much we extend and improve people's external lives through expo-nential breakthroughs, the only thing that will bring about real change is dealing with and rewiring our internal pro-gramming. Otherwise, no amount of change will ever suffice. By breaking free from the habitual patterns of suffering, the things we have become so accustomed to, we can reclaim our innate capacity to be "on purpose" and as a result be more impactful in the world.

LEONARD

My friend Leonard believed his purpose was to create technology that would transform the lives of others. He was often disappointed because much of the technology he helped create didn't have the impact he was hoping for. Some of the companies he worked with took a differ-ent direction upon funding, while others were downright flops. This apparent lack of success ate away at his sense of purpose, and Leonard was constantly doubting himself, thinking he had so much more to offer.

I asked Leonard to express the qualities he experienced when he felt "on purpose." He closed his eyes, smiled, and came up with things like, "Service-oriented, fully alive, inspired, and creative." Realizing these were all internal experiences he could embody independent of his current job, whether or not the technology he created reached people the way he had intended, was empowering for him. He also realized the more he embodied those values, the more he was able to show up fully in whatever he was doing. As he did, he felt that his unique expression in the world mattered. He was no longer outsourcing his purposefulness. By taking full responsibility for his "how," he transformed his relationship with his work and, more importantly, himself.

THE OUTER AND INNER WORLDS

We are living in the most abundant time the world has ever known. Now, more than ever, information and services are just a click away. No matter how exciting that is, we also live in a time when depression, anxiety, inequality, stress, anger, hostility, loneliness, and isolation are pervasive. How can we be so connected and so alone, so empowered and so debilitated, all at the same time?

Modern advances have changed all our lives dramatically, but somehow our inner world hasn't kept up. Our operating system is still stuck on survival mode. Of course, we have evolved culturally and socially, but our brains and nervous systems haven't really changed from the days when most of our attention was focused on avoiding catastrophe. Even when there is no real reason for our brain to be on high alert, it finds something, anything, to ruminate about. It doesn't deal well with the status quo, because it has been trained to be on the constant lookout for what's wrong. It pays more attention to what's not working than developing an appreciation for what is. Psychologists refer to this as negativity bias.

The brains of humans and other animals contain a mechanism that is designed to give priority to bad news...this circuit improves the animal's odds of living long enough to reproduce.
—DANIEL KAHNEMAN, Author: *Thinking, Fast and Slow*, Nobel Memorial Prize in Economic Sciences (2002)

Sure, this was relevant when we had to hunt and gather in order to survive. Today, all we have to do is walk over to the supermarket and put items into a shopping cart. For most of us, our existence no longer depends on constantly looking for what's wrong.

JOHNNY

My friend Johnny was one of the most successful business-men in all of Latin America. Managing thousands of em-ployees, he made multimillion-dollar decisions every day. Impacts from his actions were felt throughout his country and beyond. Johnny was constantly stressed. Stuck in a constant state of anxiety, he had difficulty sleeping and was rarely present for friends and family.

When Johnny retired, he believed it would be the end of this dysfunctional behavior. He thought he would finally relax. But, like the rest of us, Johnny's brain was never trained to unwind. He never really learned or practiced a sense of calm. Although Johnny's outer world changed with his retirement, his inner world remained on high alert. He experienced the same level of stress and anxiety, only now his problems were as mundane as his internet being slow or a barista not preparing his coffee just the right way. For him, running out of dishwasher soap became a major crisis. Johnny understood how irrational all this was and the toll it was taking on him, but he didn't know how to stop overreacting. He spoke about it as a subtle form of PTSD.

His system, like most of ours, needed some rewiring. The first step, as always, was bringing awareness into the pattern by slowing things down. He became intentional about noticing every time he was triggered. He began to recognize there was a common denominator to all these reactive moments, a sense of urgency.

In his career, Johnny was dealing with emergencies all the time, or, using the metaphor he used, "putting out fires." Even though he retired, he never quit his firefighting duties. We tried an exercise where he would visualize all these triggering events as little fires. After imagining them as flames, he would begin calming his system through conscious breathing. He would then ask, "Is this fire growing out of control? Is there urgency to it?" Ninety-nine percent of the time the answer was no. This started to chip away at the reactive pattern and allowed his programming to regulate to a new reality, one where he could consciously respond to things. He wasn't able to always catch the habit, but he interrupted it enough times that it began to lose its grip and power over him. Last time I saw Johnny, he was truly enjoying retirement and he was a much more "selective firefighter."

Although few of us are as wealthy and influential as Johnny, I think we can all relate to his dilemma. We irrationally over-react to problems that are often trivial, whether it's someone honking at us on the freeway or a loved one speaking to us in a certain tone of voice.

RESISTANCE AND ACCEPTANCE

One of my favorite spiritual teachers, Byron Katie, says that suffering is our resistance to *what is*. I've never heard a clearer definition for suffering. My experience is that I suffer any time I resist life. I used to think I needed to resist in order to overcome. If I didn't, I would become passive and unable to take action, and nothing would ever change. But acceptance does not mean complacency, passivity, or even indifference. Whenever I operate from resistance, my judg-ment (of whatever it is that I am resisting) places a burden on my organic ability to act effectively. When I'm able to accept whatever is happening, within or outside myself, my capacity to discern the situation and take appropriate action is much greater because I am not encumbered by judgment.

BOB

My friend Bob believed acceptance somehow meant giving up and sitting back. When his wife became ill, he thought, "How can I accept that my wife is sick and may die? It's like I am giving up on her." I was able to support Bob in realizing the way he was approaching his wife's illness wasn't helpful. Throwing our arms up in despair is detachment, not acceptance. When situations like this arrive, having thoughts like, "Why is this happening?" or "This shouldn't be happening," are actually detrimental to our capacity to show up when someone needs us most. Because of these thoughts, Bob was stressed and negative toward everything, including his wife's doctors. He blamed himself for not being able to help her.

His resistance was getting in the way of his resourcefulness and hindering his capacity to deal with the situation. More importantly, it was getting in the way of his ability to connect with her at this critical time. Acceptance says, "OK, this is happening. How do I move forward from here?" This takes enormous courage because we have to drop resistance, whose game is to justify its existence by making us think, "If I don't resist or judge, nothing will happen." But that hasn't always been my experience. Bob had the courage to stop resisting.

At first, strong emotions came up for him. He hadn't really cried about what was happening to his wife until that moment. Judging the doctors, the situation, and ultimately complaining about it all were ways in which he was avoiding feeling tremendous sadness. It seemed easier for him to focus outward than to let himself feel what he was really feeling. Bob also believed that experiencing sadness was self-indulgent and a waste of precious time. In finally meeting that hurt, something in Bob shifted. With tears in his eyes, he looked up, tried to smile, and said, "I just love her so much."

From that place, the question then became: how does that love show up? A renewed sense of energy washed over Bob. All he wanted to do was go hug his wife, not because she was sick, but because he loved her.

A few weeks later, I reached out to Bob to follow up. He reflected on how much things had changed since we were last together. While he was still sad and struggling with the reality of his wife's illness, he said he was finally able to be there emotionally for her. He was no longer resisting the illness and still felt incredibly driven to do all he could in order to help. He informed me about all the articles he had read and all the appointments he had made for his wife. As a result, his relationship with his wife's doctors was also transformed. This was love in action.

IT'S ALL PERSPECTIVE

Living in Los Angeles, California, means traffic is on our minds a lot of the time. I think we can all relate to traffic jams as ripe soil for resistance. Inside of a traffic jam, the first impulse is to resist *what is*. We want the cars to move faster, but they don't. We tell ourselves stories, blame anyone and everyone around us, including the government, for creating this terrible situation, and then judge ourselves for getting on the road at the wrong time or not taking some other route or other mode of transportation.

A traffic jam can be incredibly grueling for as long as we are in it. However, we all instinctively know that shifting to acceptance of our situation will ultimately open us up to a completely different frame of mind. We may not get to move any faster by accepting *what is,* but our trip will be less miserable and perhaps even more enjoyable when we do. I'm sure everyone has seen that one driver who doesn't seem to mind the slug-like pace of a traffic jam. They might even be in full karaoke mode rocking out while behind the wheel. And there we are, manically swerving from lane to lane and then back again while narrowly avoiding collision, only to end up right next to that joyful guy who hasn't moved lanes or popped a vein in misery.

When we resist, we are simply trying to get *free from* whatever we consider undesirable and unpleasant. The thing we seem to forget is the events and experiences we try to avoid are undesirable, not in and of themselves, but because of how we choose to relate to them. Think about a rainstorm. It isn't unpleasant or undesirable until we create a story about how it impacts us negatively. Negative emotions persist within us only because we persist in interpreting them as negative. While one person might see a rainstorm as horrible, another might view it as liquid sunshine and choose to go out and sing in the rain. For this, all we have to do is look to our children for guidance. When it rains, little kids want to go out and start jumping in puddles. No amount of effort or struggle will make it stop raining, so why not adjust our relationship to what is and join in on the fun?

The moment that judgement stops through acceptance
of what is, you are free of the mind. You have made room
for love, for joy, for peace.
—ECKHART TOLLE, Spiritual teacher and author

In today's society, we have become relatively adept at shielding ourselves from experiencing what we don't want to experience. This can include avoiding people who trigger us or closing off emotionally altogether. There is a whole movement encouraging people to surround themselves with people who uplift them. While there is nothing wrong with that, it can often be just another way of putting blame out there. "They bring me down, so I'll avoid them." There are certainly times when keeping our distance from particular individuals is appropriate, but more often than not, this is used as a hall pass for our ego to judge and not take responsibility. If that's the case, we are again outsourcing our well-being by conditioning it to how others show up. If someone has the power to bring us up, then they have the power to bring us down.

In 2018, I went to the Burning Man festival for the first time. For years, I had heard about the event but chose not to attend. When I finally said yes, I never expected to learn about myself as much as I did. If you aren't familiar with Burning Man, the festival takes place in an isolated spot in the Nevada desert in late August. This is one of the hottest times of the year in the western US, especially in the desert. Not only is it incredibly hot during the day, it's also really cold at night. That's the duality of the desert. To top it off, intense sandstorms arrive without warning. I'm not sure if you have ever been in a sandstorm, but they are blinding and can feel like you are being hit with a sandblaster if you are caught in the middle of one of them.

During one particular sandstorm, I found myself stepping outside five different times to try to patch the windows on my RV with duct tape. Every time I stepped outside, I seemed to grunt a little louder, especially when the sand pelted my face and clothing. Desert sand isn't like the sand you find at the beach. It's smaller grained and dusty. It was coming in through the smallest of openings of the RV, flooding everything inside with the fine powder of desert dust. I was in total resistance to what was happening. My eyes could only half open, so I couldn't really see anything. My hair was white from the sand, and my skin was cracking like old paint on a fence. To make matters worse, the tape wouldn't stick to the windows I was trying to seal because with every strip I pulled from the roll, sand would attach to the sticky side of the tape. I was literally fighting the environment and losing. Badly.

Fortunately, somewhere between eating sand and rubbing my eyes raw with all the micro-dust flying around, I snapped out of it. A small, subtle smile started to form on the sides of my mouth. The silliness of my approach to what was happening finally hit me. To think my resistance was helping in any way or that the sandstorm cared about my complaining became amusing to me. Recognizing and yielding to what was actually happening, I started to laugh out loud. I began having fun with the crazy sandstorm and ridiculous situation before me. I can only imagine what people thought of me, laughing and yelling as I was pummeled with sheets of sand.

Strangely enough—or perhaps, not so strangely—with this newly adopted attitude, I was able to figure out what I needed to do. I could pay attention to the gusts of wind and time the opening of my eyes to effectively apply tape in between the intense gusts. Prior to that, the wind had seemed like one big, continuous tornado. Now, I accepted what was happening and shifted my perspective into one of cooperation, despite all the discomfort and unfolding chaos from the wind. While I enjoyed going to Burning Man that one time, it's not something I'm necessarily inclined to do anytime soon. Acceptance at its finest.

CHAPTER 4

○

WHAT IS POSSIBLE

Shifting our default mode from surviving to thriving is easier than most of us imagine. There are practical tools, which we were never taught, that can help us unravel our conditioning and misunderstandings so we can experience this kind of freedom. A way of living that is in alignment with our innermost being, or soul, if you will, just feels good. We just have to be willing to question the way in which we have been operating.

I used to think I needed to choose between living in the world of mortgages, relationships, taxes, homework, etc. and a life of inner peace. I was convinced if I wanted this type of freedom, my life had to be perfectly solved or I had to choose a very different lifestyle. Fortunately, that was just one more way in which the ego attempted to lock in the status quo. The joy and peace once thought to be reserved for ashrams and monasteries is actually available to us all.

MAKING SUFFERING OPTIONAL

It is impossible to escape pain or sadness. I can't begin to tell you how hard I have tried. I have now come to embrace them as essential ingredients in this human soup we call our life. We would love to keep the pendulum forever on the side of joy and bliss, but, sooner or later, the pendulum's nature is to swing back and slap us around from time to time. There is, however, a possibility for peace within these pendulum swings. That is when suffering becomes optional.

It's important to remember there is a difference between pain or hurt and suffering. I may be sad when I see my child hurting physically or emotionally. Maybe she had a fall at school, or maybe someone said something mean to her. In situations like this, my heart may ache. With that said, I could also go through the same experience, adding the thought or belief that my child shouldn't have been hurt, and go on the attack with thoughts like, "Who did this to my daughter? This shouldn't have happened! Teachers should be more on top of things."

All these beliefs about what should be happening or what should not be happening are the cause of our suffering. I could easily justify them, saying they stem from my love for my daughter, but I'm actually acting out of self-interest. When I look closely, I realize I was feeling bad because my daughter was feeling bad. I wanted her to feel better so I could feel better.

I never would have imagined that something like parenting, which seems so selfless on the surface, had the potential to be so self-oriented. My judgment about what had happened was really my resistance to experiencing a heartache born purely out of my love for her. As Byron Katie so eloquently reminds us, suffering is resistance to life. When we resist what is, we lose. If you don't resist what is actually happening, even though your heart is with your child when she is hurt, or you are in pain because your body is ill, you won't suffer.

When I first heard this, I was skeptical. Not too long afterward, I had an intense headache and put it to the test. It was as if someone had placed a jackhammer inside of my head. It was insanely painful. My initial reaction to the jackhammer was to resist the sensation. A familiar stream of consciousness began first with the past: "What did I do to make this happen? Did I hit my head somewhere? What did I eat? Did I sleep crooked last night?" When I found no satisfying answers, fact or fiction, my focus shifted to the future: "When will the pain stop? Should I take medicine? This is so inconvenient, because I have a dinner tonight." It was interesting to notice the rush of ideas. Within a matter of seconds, I had a myriad of thoughts, which all stemmed from resistance.

As the jackhammer persisted, I remembered Katie's invitation for me to not resist. The intention by itself created enough space for the constant flow of thoughts to stop. I was confused, though. I mean, how do I stop wanting this to go away when it feels like my brain is imploding? Suddenly I came to the awareness that I was actually resisting my current resistance to the headache. Yeah, I know. I was confused too. But, in a moment of grace, I dropped all of my "thinking" strategies to make something happen, even the "conscious" strategy to stop my resistance to the resistance. I became present with what was true in that moment. Yes, there was an intense pain in my head. Yes, there was an undeniable desire for the pain to stop. My question now was this: could I accept all of it?

When I finally accepted what was happening (the pain and my desire for it to stop), my approach to the whole situation shifted. I became curious about the pain itself. What did it feel like? What sensations did it cause within my body? How was my breath? It turns out, my sense of wonder and curiosity was the antidote to all the resistance. I was embracing the sensation through exploration, instead of simply pushing it away. I felt the pressure in my temples and the desire for it to subside, but somehow the experience became a lot less bothersome. That's not to say I wouldn't still choose to take aspirin if the situation merited, but there was now enough space to consider it as an option, not a given. I was fascinated at how simple it was to shift out of suffering by simply paying attention to what was happening. This allowing, even if that included making space for my nonacceptance, was freeing.

Like a mad scientist whose crazy experiment was finally proven, I quickly began testing it on everything. To date, I haven't found a situation where resistance proved to be a better strategy than acceptance. Now, I don't expect you to take this or anything I say as a scientific fact. I simply hope that you give it a try.

HURDLES AS BREADCRUMBS

Life can get bumpy, so we might as well use the challenges we encounter along the way to support our growth. I use everything that disturbs me as a pointer. My upsets are invitations to look at areas in my life that require attention. Some of the biggest triggers for people come from family, close friends, romantic partners, and business relationships. Proximity has the ability to bring up high levels of resistance at the drop of a hat. The reason they push our buttons is because they are simply close enough to push them. Remember, it's not personal; they're just mirrors. In the case of intimate relationships, they're more like those vanity mirrors that enhance every little pore in your face.

Our wounds and self-judgments have the ability to hide, but the closer someone is, the more exposed these sensitive areas are. At times others may see things in us that we have learned to ignore, because we don't like them ourselves, that can be even more triggering. From an early age, we learn and implement a series of trapdoors and coping mechanisms, which ultimately divert us from actually dealing with the places that hurt. These avoidance strategies try to keep us from hurting again, but they end up becoming the fixations that perpetuate our suffering. Blame and self-judgment are two of the most common ways we avoid dealing with our unresolved issues. They keep us in the story of "there's something wrong with them" or "there's something wrong with me." In the end, however, they are just ineffective ways we learned to deal with our hurt.

The ego is very invested in all those stories; it doesn't like taking responsibility and breaking old habits. It knows how to be the victim or judge (blame here or blame there) and has an opinion about everything and everyone. We've been operating in the same way for so long that some of these thoughts and reactions happen very fast, almost immediately. That's why we have to slow things down again. I hope you're seeing a pattern here. We first bring awareness, then acceptance, and then let course correction follow.

JAMES

About twenty years ago, my friend James founded a company with a friend of his. Recently, James discovered that his "friend" had been taking money out of the business from day one. Livid, James confided in me by asking, "How could he betray me after all I have done for him? I trusted him with my life." His anger and blame eventually turned into self-judgment: "Why didn't I see this coming? I should've known! How could I have been so stupid?"

Beneath the anger, James was actually feeling the pain of his friend's betrayal. From an early age, however, he was conditioned to avoid certain feelings. It's not because the anger and judgment are more comfortable than sadness, it's because they seemed (unconsciously) safer and more bearable to him.

James was stuck on surface-level emotions: blaming, shaming, and victimizing. This painful incident was keeping him up at night and completely overwhelming his life. James's pain had turned into suffering. He couldn't snap out of it because he was committed to holding on to his story and internalizing it.

When we latch on to a position of righteousness, it's like we are stuck between a rock and a hard place. We want to get out, but some part of us doesn't want to move. This is why I invited James to question the belief that he needed to be angry in order to address the situation and ultimately take care of himself. He was receptive enough to recognize the anger wasn't absolutely necessary. It was justified, of course, but not necessary. Through this simple acknowledgment, his mind became more still, and sadness found an opening. Underneath anger there's hurt, and beneath hurt there's care. James was able to stay out of the roller coaster of his mind long enough to connect with the hurt and eventually the love underneath it all. He genuinely loved his partner and the business they had created together. He was tremendously sad because he cared so deeply. Caring, by definition, involves taking a risk. His heart was broken.

It is a risk to care, because life has a tendency to not go according to plan. We will inevitably experience loss. But that doesn't and shouldn't stop us from caring. In that moment, James refused to let this love become tainted by his partner's lack of integrity.

This didn't mean James was excusing his partner's actions. Not at all. He was simply recognizing that there was a different way of "being" with the situation within himself. He was even able to look at how he had played a role in what had happened. By avoiding difficult conversations and not confronting his partner when some things weren't adding up financially, he remained complicitly silent. This was a pattern in James's life.

James went on to take legal action and do what he needed to do to protect himself financially. However, his actions and state of being with the problem were no longer encumbered by anger and self-judgment. He had stopped suffering, which enabled him to act more effectively and efficiently.

Holding on to anger is like grasping a hot coal with the intent of throwing it at someone else; you are the one who gets burned.
—BUDDHA

THE ILLUSION OF CONTROL

One of the greatest egoic delusions is that we have control over what's happening; we really don't. Just notice how quickly something like COVID-19 can humble us. Like most unexpected life events, it shows us the fragility of all that we hold dear—of all those plans and ideas we had of what was going to happen. A virus reminded the world of the illusion of control.

When we look closely, we realize that most things, like the weather, world events, and a pandemic, are obviously out of our control. However, we still believe that we're in control of our immediate reality. I would like to challenge that perception. We are certainly not in control of how our heart is beating right now or the next thought that might pop into our head. We have limited control over pretty much everything; just think of today. How much control did you have over your sleep or in determining your mood upon waking and every little thing that's happened since then? When we convince ourselves that we are in control and craft perfect scenarios of how things are going to turn out, more often than not, we end up disappointed. These expectations are one of the main reasons we suffer. We can make plans, but life just shows up the way it shows up. It rains on our wedding day, our children get sick, or we get stuck in traffic on the way to an important meeting. Life is constantly showing us that the belief that we're in charge is nothing more than our ego's wishful thinking.

Our desire to control what happens in life is ultimately, and inevitably, self-defeating. We might have the best intentions, but for something to have the effect we would like requires that a lot of pieces out of our domain fall into perfect place. We are essentially pretending we know what should be happening, even though our capacity to understand all the elements at play is clearly limited. It sounds silly, but we often act as if we have godlike omniscience and total knowledge of what the best thing for ourselves and everyone else involved ought to be.

How often have we been surprised by something that happens when we thought it was the last thing we wanted to happen? These surprises, difficult as they may seem, often have equally unexpected benefits, not necessarily immediately, but often over time. A mind that is open enough to know it doesn't really know what's best is more creative, curious, and ultimately a freer and happier mind.

Not that long ago, an amazing soccer player, a goalie, was being touted as a candidate for his country's national team. Then, at nineteen, he was involved in a car accident that left him paralyzed from the chest down, a paralysis that would see him bedridden for over two years. His soccer career was over. The goalie was distraught, and nothing could lift his spirits. One day, a nurse who was treating him brought him a guitar. She figured it would be a distraction from the depression and a way to gain dexterity and strength in his fingers and hands.

He began playing guitar in the hospital and continued when he got home throughout his recovery. The goalie's mind must've been open enough because, through music, he reconnected with his aliveness. He never went back to playing soccer, but he did become a famous musician. His name is Julio Iglesias.

IMPERMANENCE

While at times we might be convinced that the storm we are in will last forever, it won't. It never has. An Eastern sage was asked by his sultan to inscribe on a ring the sentiment which would always be true and appropriate, no matter the situation. He engraved on it the words, "And this, too, shall pass away."

No experience we have ever had, will have, or could ever have can remain the same. When I let this idea really sink in, it had transformative implications on my life. I started to notice how everything I had done up until that point was based on trying to arrive somewhere, as if happiness were a destination. I wanted to avoid all the bad events and only experience safety, comfort, recognition, and joy, believing if I made the right choices, those positive experiences would prevail. That sounded like freedom, but it was actually a form of bondage. By definition, freedom doesn't put restrictions on life or condition our well-being to a particularly desired experience. It is free even when things are not going our way.

Living from that place requires us to release the world from our expectations and attachments. We can still set goals and have objectives, but we can do that while embodying a sense of well-being that is independent of life going one way or another. A perspective like this, however, is counter to our conditioning, so it requires us to pay close attention.

This process starts by exploring what is true for ourselves and getting curious with our direct experience of any given moment. One way I like to do this is by taking a deep breath and settling into the exhale. I can always count on my breath to get grounded and take me out of the trance of time. What would it be like, for example, if right now, for just a brief period, you suspended any demand on life? What if you opened your mind to the possibility that, right now, everything was just as it was supposed to be? Can you let go of all your ideas of what should be different and allow your shoulders and belly to relax? Even a few seconds of letting your system recognize the inherent tranquility that comes from not having a personal agenda, no matter how subtle, can disrupt the pattern of inner chaos. What is it like to be here neutrally as a witness to whatever is happening?

Asking these kinds of questions can give us a glimpse into the simplicity of existence we may recall from childhood. I used to think it was impossible to live from a place like that. I imagined nothing would ever happen and saw future images of a catatonic me sitting on a couch all day long. Nothing could be further from the truth, though, that peace is pure kinetic energy and is incredibly alive.

No matter how different we may appear to one another from the outside, on the inside, we are each running the same software and core misunderstandings. My hope is that individually and collectively we are finally ready to embrace a way of being that is more natural for us—a new way of seeing each other and, most importantly, ourselves.

THE ELUSIVE PRESENT

Why is it so hard to be present, though? And if we're not here, where are we? According to Harvard psychologists Matthew Killingsworth and Daniel Gilbert, the human mind is in a state of continuous distraction. Their studies concluded that we spend around 47 percent of our time "mind wandering." Mind wandering is a more academic way of saying "checked out." They suggest we spend half our day in fantasyland. I'm not as optimistic. I think that most of the other half is not really spent being present either.

Even when we're not daydreaming, we're likely still engaged in thoughts of past and future, memory, and anticipation. That's why something as natural as just being can be so challenging.

I remember going to retreats or workshops and having the intention to be present; it was hard work. My mind was turning "being present" into some kind of to-do. Minds love to have goals. "I'm going to do all these things so that I become present." Our to-dos, however, happen in the future. Presence, by definition, only happens here. "I must be present" became the new way I tried to control what was going to happen. In striving to stop my mind and the busyness of my thoughts, I was just perpetuating the "something must change" dilemma.

When I hear people struggle with this, I suggest they stop trying to be present. Any approach that tells us something is wrong with this current moment simply prolongs the same thought patterns and beliefs we are trying to evolve out of. No matter how lost we are in thinking about the future or reminiscing about the past, we are always here and there has never been an exception. There is nothing other than this moment. The mind may focus on the future, but there is nowhere to be other than right here. Our thoughts function in time, yet direct experience always happens here and now. If we're always here, though, why do we rarely feel present?

THE MIDDLEMAN

Instead of directly experiencing life, we've become experts at interpreting and labeling whatever is happening. It's as if we've placed a dividing line between us and our experiences, both inner and outer. This concocted layer of consciousness is where our relationship to *what is* resides. This is the realm of our inner narrator. You know the one that always has something to say: "I like this. This is too hot. I don't like this. I should be more present. I should be more successful."

The ability to reflect on and assess the situation before us is a valuable tool. Unfortunately, we have made it our de facto state. We have turned this analytical instrument into our way of life. When we are fully present, this eager commentator fades and sometimes, even temporarily, disappears. We become one with the moment and there is no longer a person being present, there is just presence. The barrier between us and the environment thins, and our ideas of what should or shouldn't be stop being so relevant. In the absence of that self-reflective chatter, we experience a deeper intimacy with life.

Some people call this a state of flow. They experience it while jogging, gardening, dancing, painting, and so forth. Some of us may have experienced this deep presence in moments of awe, like watching a beautiful sunset or the miracle of childbirth. If we pay close enough attention, we notice we don't label these profound moments while they are happening, but only after the fact. "Wow, that was wonderful. I had a great run. I got lost in the moment back there. What a deep meditation!" The middleman is back in business with an opinion about everything, putting us somewhere other than here and now.

We might think we lost the oneness, but it hasn't gone anywhere. It is just as accessible here and now as it has ever been. But when we try to turn the "now" into what was, we are sure to miss it. What made this deep presence and joy accessible in the first place was that the "me" stepped back as the moment's protagonist and left us with an unedited discovery of life. When we try to replicate the moment, we're back in the business of manipulating and controlling, instead of simply noticing it. We are like babies hoping to see the picture at the bottom of a basin by moving the water around. The picture is effortlessly revealed when we stop trying to look for it by sloshing the water. When the water becomes still, we see the picture. We are trying to get to "what's happening now" in the only way we've been taught, by making it happen. Sometimes, just *being* reveals what all that *doing* couldn't.

CHAPTER 5

○

DYNAMIC SURRENDER

When we try to control what's happening, we are essentially saying, "I know better what this moment should be like. Even though there are billions of preferences and they're all likely different, mine is the right one." I've met some incredibly devout Christians who wholeheartedly recite, "Thy will be done," but actually have strict demands on how things *should* be. When we try to control existence, we are proclaiming, "My will be done." We try to play God. Deep down, the belief is, "When what I want to happen finally happens, things will be OK, and I'll be OK."

Resisting what is happening is basically postponing our joy. Joy happens *in* the moment. "Now isn't good enough as it is, so I'll go chasing after the experience I want and not really be here." It is possible, however, to go after what we want and still be totally here. As a way of bringing this into awareness, I often invite people who are anxious to get somewhere to remember a time in the past when they felt most complete.

NICOLE

Nicole is an entrepreneur I have had the pleasure of working with. She is not only smart but incredibly driven. Her two previous startups achieved good outcomes, but not to the degree she hoped for. Now, she was on her third company and working harder than ever. She was confident this was the "big one," but she was also tired and a little burnt out from her previous ventures. She felt like there had to be a different way of going about it but just couldn't see it. When I asked how she would feel after the big win, she took a deep breath, lingered for a moment, and said with a smile, "Relaxed, joyful, and content."

Surprisingly, the last time she remembered feeling this way was when she was a kid, playing on the swings at the park. She smiled, because she hadn't thought of that moment in years. With her eyes closed, she started recalling the details of the experience. I watched as her body slowly relaxed, her face softened, and her energy shifted entirely. She began to embody the sense of relaxation and contentment she was looking to feel again with the success of her company, simply by thinking of her time at the park. Nothing in her world had changed and it was the memory that had elicited the experience, but the joy and peace were happening in the now. Nicole was treating herself to the carrot without chasing after it.

When Nicole opened her eyes back up, she was still smiling, but then her mind started to kick back in. She looked confused and, as if looking for permission, asked, "Can I just do that all the time?" To many of us, it almost feels like heresy to enjoy something without having first earned it. For some dysfunctional reason, we believe we need to struggle first in order to really deserve to feel good.

Nicole was skeptical, though. She couldn't imagine how experiencing that joy and contentment along the way would coexist with her drive and desire to grow her company. I knew she wasn't going to take my word for it, so I invited her to test it out. She decided to run the experiment for a couple days, as anything more felt risky. We connected a month afterward and it turns out the experiment was still going. She shared how she was working harder than ever, but there was a lot more ease in her life. Nicole still experienced moments of anxiety, but she now had an image of a swing set at her desk, which reminded her to take a beat and embody what she really desired, whenever she wanted to.

To illustrate how powerful the mind can be, visualize a ripe, juicy, yellow lemon and then imagine cutting it and putting a piece of it in your mouth, rind and all. Imagine biting down as the acid sweetness of the lemon juice trickles down the sides of your mouth. The thought alone can illicit the immediate secretion of the saliva glands. Even when the lemon is merely a thought, the body reacts because it can't tell the difference.

It is quite humbling to realize how vulnerable our body is to the thoughts running through our minds. Unfortunately, we have inherited the tendency to focus on looming threats. It's no wonder there's so much anxiety and stress, and therefore disease, in our world. We need to stop hanging out in a negative fantasyland, because our bodies are responding in kind.

Your brain and body don't know the difference between having an actual experience in your life and just thinking about the experience...neuro-chemically, it's the same.
—DR. JOE DISPENZA, Neuroscientist,
Author: *You Are the Placebo: Making Your Mind Matter*

Even though the choice to become an entrepreneur requires a tremendous and unrelenting sense of optimism, many of the individuals I have mentored or have chosen to invest in continue to operate from this negative filter. There seems to be a shared belief that it is the job or responsibility of an entrepreneur to always worry. It is not. Through misguided thinking or lack of confidence, they believe it would be a breach of their fiduciary responsibility to relax in the process of creating what they have envisioned. As their investor, I give them a hall pass to question if this is true or not. It is funny to see how reluctant some of them are at first, because it is the opposite of their conditioning. Thankfully, most of them eventually realize they can be much better stewards and managers from a state of inner calm than from a place of contraction and concern.

The thing I find interesting is that both CEOs of large, established companies and founders of early startups often face the same issues. The size of their businesses or where they are in their careers may vary, but it doesn't really make a difference in how much they worry or how hard they turn the screws for results. They've been trained to be concerned and run "in pursuit" at all times and feel that, if they stop, things will fall apart.

BRENT

One such CEO is my friend Brent. In his early sixties, Brent ran a multibillion-dollar conglomerate which touched millions of lives. He always believed there was a big event just around the corner that would finally allow him to take a breather and enjoy life. Ever since his kids were in elementary school, he had committed to getting his life in balance, shortly. That "shortly" delay meant as soon as whatever was going on with the business was sorted out.

With his kids now in college, I invited Brent to explore what goal he would need to reach in order to prioritize the balance he had been postponing. Brent quickly recited a list of well-thought-out benchmarks. These benchmarks were probably taken straight out of his recent report to Wall Street. I asked him what he thought he would have answered to the same question ten years ago. He smiled, catching on to where I was directing him. He had already blown way past his objectives in the last ten years, but there was no stopping in sight. He trusted me enough to admit he was caught and acknowledged that there would always be a new set of goals, benchmarks, or achievements. He was able to notice the times he had almost gotten there, but how, when new challenges inevitably emerged, he chose to press on to the next hurdle.

As obvious as that was, he had never really slowed down enough to recognize that the self-imposed finish line had become something of a moving target. Brent was very sharp, and his mind was quick as a whistle. It always seemed like he was going a million miles an hour, but, in that moment, Brent was able to shift into a more spacious, integrated, and receptive way of being. He took a deep breath and smiled. It almost seemed like his system was remembering what peace felt like. Now, you wouldn't be able to tell from the way he moved through life, but Brent really wanted to slow down and enjoy things.

He knew running so fast was unsustainable, but he was afraid the business would suffer if he didn't somehow keep pace. Finding the courage, he committed to a week of building in more of the life balance he kept postponing and decided to put it to the test. As you can see, I always invite people to test things out for themselves, because what works for one person might not work for another. When the skeptical parts of our selves are able to witness what is possible, the integration of new habits is much easier.

Brent's week-long experiment turned into a month. His employees started to notice a shift in the way Brent was showing up. While he still pushed them and set very ambitious benchmarks, they recognized that something was indeed different. The results from his quarterly 360 review, a process through which his employees gave him feedback, noted that he was more available to listen, was more approachable, and wasn't as narrowly focused or judgmental as he had seemed before. What appeared at first to be just a stress-relief mechanism soon yielded some incredible business results. Brent and his team were able to reconnect with the inspiration and creativity they had had when they first began. Somewhere along the way, the inspiration was replaced with long hours and a culture of overworking. Brent realized he had forgotten why he was doing what he was doing. Because he was so intensely focused on the next win, Brent had lost his joy of being.

Brent's company eventually hit the benchmark it was aiming for. A lavish celebration followed to celebrate the win. And while they had had "big wins" and celebrations in the past, these had always been short-lived and bittersweet. As soon as the celebration had ended, they had quickly set a new goal or benchmark. Before the champagne bubbles had settled, everyone had gone back to the grind. This time was different. They weren't simply celebrating the latest win, they were celebrating their new working culture. Through his own transformation, Brent was able to share a new way of being—an invitation to do business from a more enjoyable place. This enjoyment was possible because it was no longer outsourced to a later date when they hit a target, benchmark, or goal.

Creativity needs space to bloom. There are situations where linear thinking is incredibly valuable and others that benefit from a larger aperture. Sometimes, when we seek out creativity, we have a tendency to stomp on the soil and demand results. We all want to be inspired, but moments of ingenuity typically arrive without expectations or conditions.

Creativity is the language of curiosity. As Albert Einstein put it, "No problem can be solved from the same level of consciousness that created it." Sometimes all we really need to do is stop what we are doing and allow wonder and contemplation to guide us. Then, we lean into it.

THE CARROT AND THE BAG OF SHIT

A kōan is a story, question, or statement which is used in Zen practice to provoke the "great doubt." It is used to practice or test a student's progress in Zen Buddhism. One particular kōan has been adapted to consist of a simple stick-figure diagram of someone with a pole attached to the top of their head. At one end of the pole is a carrot in front of the person's face. On the other end of the pole is a bag of shit. This carrot is accomplishment, the place of arrival, and the moment of being fully acknowledged and appreciated. It is whatever motivates us and fuels our desires. The bag of shit represents everything that we fear or whatever we are trying to outrun or avoid.

In business, the carrot can be a promotion, the next big deal, or a company being acquired. In relationships, it can be finding the right partner or getting that partner to show up in a certain way. With children, it can represent finally mastering this thing called "parenting." In the domain of self-improvement, it can be finally meeting our ideals. The carrot is what we strive for in every aspect of our lives.

Internally speaking, the carrot can represent things like happiness, love, or joy, and the bag of shit is guilt, regret, or anxiety. This is the fuel that keeps us running toward what we want or running away from what we don't. In the end, we are caught in a self-fulfilling dilemma. The pole is attached to our heads and has an infinite supply of carrots and shit. So, if we still operate with the belief that our well-being depends on getting "there" and outrunning "this or that," we won't ever shift out of this draining paradigm. No matter how much we run, how many wins we obtain, or how much shit we might avoid, we keep running.

This push-pull fuel is certainly powerful but extremely taxing. It uses the unquestioned assumption that our survival is at stake or on the verge of threat. We can usually recognize when this fuel is driving us because we are incredibly attached to our agenda. This is perpetuated by the idea that once we get "there" our lives will be fine, and we'll finally be able to enjoy things. This is the "happily ever after" fantasy. We are equally convinced that if that stinky bag of shit hits us and the worst-case scenario unfolds, our world will truly end.

When we get the big win or recognition we have been waiting for, there's a moment of satisfaction and arrival, because succeeding makes us feels good. The mind is trained to register change, so it likes arriving, but it perceives resting for too long as dangerous, which is why we are never satisfied. Driven personalities even associate the absence of this quick-burning fuel with stagnation and depression. We've stopped our arduous climb and find ourselves on a plateau, but we've become infatuated with the effort of climbing. We become addicted to wanting to get there, so we quickly look for the next rung on the ladder. For those of us who may be growth oriented, it's valuable to clarify the distinction between climbing because we love to climb and doing it because there's a bear chasing us. Running for survival keeps us very attached and restricted. It wears our system down. Being fueled by inspiration and creativity is self-replenishing and a lot more enjoyable.

ROOTED HERE

A lot of the friends I have had the pleasure of mentoring admit the one thing they love the most is closing a deal. "I love a challenge and making things happen." Those same individuals, however, recognize there's a difference between the drive that comes from enthusiasm and the one that is entangled with an attachment to a particular outcome. If we can untangle the original impulse and motivation from the overtaxing thoughts that project our well-being into the future, we can engage with whatever we're doing in a more sustainable way. It's also worth noting that the moments where growth isn't apparent are just as essential to evolution as the steep hills are.

*To take the master's journey...you also have to be willing to
spend most of your time on a plateau, to keep practicing, even
when you seem to be getting nowhere... To love the plateau is
to love what is most essential and enduring in your life.*
—GEORGE LEONARD, Author: *Mastery:
The Keys to Success and Long-Term Fulfillment*

Arriving on that plateau, no matter how small it may be, gives us an opportunity to make space and to experience what it's like not to be driven forward into the future—to be here before the next new thing kicks in. It can be like shifting from standing on our tippy-toes to rooted in the soles of our feet. If we are leaning too far forward, we need to take a step or hold on to something, so we won't fall down. It's much more empowering to take a step from a stable position, standing straight, with our feet firmly on the ground. If we are solid where we are, we can go after the new carrot even though we know it won't give us enduring satisfaction.

When the fuel of trying to avoid hard times drives us, we are in survival; there's no room for joy when we're surviving. Fear of being "tight on money" and the worry and anxiety of having financial duress is a common bag of shit. It's reasonable to do anything possible to avoid hardship, but in the process of trying to outrun it, we find ourselves experiencing the stress we were trying to originally run away from. We're committed to not feeling the strain of running out of money, so we stress out on the journey of actually making money. We've traded "stress then" for "stress now."

When we are stressed, our body goes into fight-or-flight protocol, our natural functions are demoted, and those essential for dealing with an immediate threat get prioritized. This is great when we are chased by a charging lion, because we need all our energy to survive and outrun the threat. This, however, wasn't intended to be an ongoing modus operandi for daily life.

If we are able to become aware when this energy is fueling us, we can stop, take a breath, and recognize there's a different, much more productive way of moving through our lives. As important as the next "emergency" is, odds are we'll be better at dealing with it from a centered place. By slowing down and calming our system, we create a pattern interrupt which retrains us to utilize and rely on a more grounded energy. We can make plans and set ambitious goals, but by releasing our attachment to the outcomes, we expand our capacity and willingness to pivot in response to the nudges that life normally presents. With less invested in managing for a particular scenario, we can be just as engaged but can now tap into the creative reservoir of spontaneity.

I am fortunate enough to work with a lot of good-hearted people who are committed social and political activists. It's not uncommon for people who are very driven by a cause to overexert themselves. There's a sense of urgency to what they're doing and deservedly so; there's a lot of pressing need everywhere. The altruistic argument for overworking, however, is also something worth examining. A lot of my friends who are dedicated to making real change and are solely focused "out there" end up depressed and burnt out. Outsourcing our well-being is simply unsustainable and unproductive.

The carrot many of these activists operate from is often rooted in an unresolved wound within themselves. They believe that if they fix the problem outside, their inner pain will be somehow redeemed. If they can only create enough outer impact, their struggles will have been somehow worth it. Even though inner pain is a powerful motivator and one that can illicit change, people who operate out of love, rather than judgment, have a better chance at living a more effective and fulfilling life.

I once heard Jane Goodall, the famed English primatologist and anthropologist, answer a question about what should be done to poachers. She didn't go into blaming them or shaming them for what they did; she simply said it made no sense to focus on punishment but instead on developing work alternatives for the poachers, so they don't have to kill animals to feed their families. Jane was operating from a place of internal cohesion and integration. She was interested in relieving suffering, not just for the animals she cares so much for, but for the whole. That's likely the reason why, in her eighties, she's one of the most effective and engaged activists in the world. Love and compassion are a self-replenishing fuel.

CHAPTER 6

BREAKING FREE

When a baby elephant is first trained at a circus, it is chained to a post in the ground. This makes it impossible for the baby to flee. After numerous and instinctual attempts to free itself, the baby elephant gives up. It is conditioned to the idea that it's useless to keep trying. So, when the baby elephant grows into a massive beast, a single rope around its neck causes submission. It is imprisoned not by the rope but by the conditioning of captivity. If the elephant only knew how powerful it actually was, it could liberate itself in an instant.

Like the circus elephant, we too have become accustomed to living in a prison of our own making. What imprisons us are our unquestioned beliefs and assumptions about our lives. In order to break free, we must first be willing to consider a reality beyond the confines of what we take as a given. We have to open ourselves up to the possibility that our unconditioned being is powerful beyond measure and claim our intrinsic greatness.

Our deepest fear is not that we are inadequate.
Our deepest fear is that we are powerful beyond measure.
—MARIANNE WILLIAMSON,
Bestselling author and political activist

Bringing more consciousness to the journey of life requires great courage. It entails questioning what we *think* we know and looking closer and more deeply at what life *might* be like outside the habitual frame of reference. It's the exploration of a domain beyond the egoic limitations we've been, up to this moment, living with. Some may call this self-realization, while others refer to it as a search for what is true. It is ultimately an invitation to reevaluate our lives and move forward from the greatest expression of who we are meant to be. In some ways, it is a summoning back to a primordial essence prior to all the superficial definitions we've placed on ourselves. If you are reading this book, odds are you have both received and begun to answer that invitation.

TAKING RESPONSIBILITY

Shifting out of the whirlpool of the conditioned self requires an absolute commitment to accountability. True self-improvement leaves no room for excuses; we must assume 100 percent responsibility for our lives. This is where the rubber meets the road because we have to drop our stories of blame, victimization, and excuses for why we act one way and not another.

Most of us have learned to navigate the internal havoc and stress by checking out and taking a break from everything that weighs on us. We resort to coping mechanisms such as having a drink, binge-watching TV, eating, etc. These strategies give us temporary relief from being tossed around by life, and there is nothing fundamentally wrong with them. However, continually relying on distractions or other forms of disconnection to feel better is not only disempowering but ultimately unsustainable. At some point, a lifestyle that fractures our experience is bound to catch up with us. Hopefully, at some point, we grow tired of trying to distract ourselves from the underlying cause of our stress and realize we are capable and resourceful enough to stop running. We can then turn inward and claim back our power by taking full accountability for our way of being.

Now, this doesn't mean that we should shift blame from "out there" to "in here." It simply means that we drop blame altogether so we can take full responsibility for the way we show up, independent of what is happening in our lives. Becoming aware of how we give away our power by avoiding responsibility is a critical step to deep transformation. It sounds simple, but I've seen it bring about miracles.

Dr. Ron Hulnick and Dr. Mary Hulnick are the founders of the University of Santa Monica, which specializes in the practical application of universal spiritual teachings in everyday life. One of my favorite sayings from Ron and Mary is, "Any time we say, 'I'm upset because [fill in the blank],' we're giving away our power." Take relationships, for instance. Many people spend years complaining about their partners. They keep waiting for their partner to change and justify the ways they act out in the relationship by how they perceive or misperceive how their partner shows up. But it's transformational when one or both partners are able to reclaim their ability to take responsibility and fully own their way of being.

SAMANTHA

Samantha is a friend of mine whom I also mentor from time to time. As a young mother of two children, Samantha was having a lot of conflicts with her husband. In the past, they had tried couple's therapy and even participated in relationship seminars. Nothing seemed to work. Samantha felt defeated and disappointed that her life hadn't turned out the way she wanted it to. She had decided she wasn't going to leave the marriage, because of her kids, but she was resentful and closed off from her husband. Having grown tired of waiting for him to change, she gave up on the idea of a fulfilling relationship. He wasn't the husband she wanted him to be. As a result, she would frequently take her frustration out on him.

Samantha was stuck in a victim mentality and giving away her power. She felt unhappy about her entire life, not just her marriage. She and I originally spoke about difficulties in her work, but it soon became clear that victimhood was a pattern for her, not just in her job and marriage, but also in many other areas of her life. I invited Samantha to look at the part she was playing in the equation and to see if there was any way to take full responsibility for the situation at home. The suggestion caught her by surprise, because it took a beat for her to understand what I was asking. After a few pushbacks, she finally stopped focusing on her husband and recognized how long she had been criticizing him. She also acknowledged how long it had been since she had opened her heart to him, which was exactly what she accused him of not doing. Suddenly, Samantha's disposition shifted. She felt guilty as the judgment of her husband got redirected into self-judgment.

The mind is a creature of habit. It will always look for ways to continue a pattern. Guilt is nothing more than the opposite side of the "victim" coin. Sometimes, however, all we need is a nudge to stop spinning in these "whirlpools" of blame and shame and have the space for our consciousness to claim dominion over our thoughts. Once Samantha was able to recognize the role she played in her marital problems and step out of the narrative she had created, she decided to try an experiment. Instead of delaying her good and her happiness, she would show up as if her husband had changed in the way she had been waiting for. In other words, she was going to stop being a victim and take full responsibility for the kind of wife she actually wanted to be. When we change how we show up, the world we experience has a way of responding in kind.

At first, the idea frightened Samantha, but she figured she had nothing to lose but her pride and a marriage that was already running on fumes. Any good experiment requires accountability and observation, so Samantha decided to keep a journal, not about him but about her. When we checked in about a month later, she said things were still challenging at home, but she felt happier. The following month, something really changed. Her husband recognized and acknowledged her shift in behavior and apologized for the times he had been short and uncaring with her. This level of openness and honest communication was something he hadn't done in a long time. When Samantha stopped demanding that he change, he had enough space to realize that he didn't particularly like his own behavior either.

When we take responsibility for our own way of being, the shift allows others to take responsibility for theirs. This frame of mind doesn't just set you free, it sets the whole world free. Taking responsibility and acting from our highest truth becomes a catalyst for everyone's transformation. Samantha had the courage to claim how she was showing up in her marriage. The fact that her husband responded by taking his own share of responsibility is great, but even if things hadn't worked out, Samantha was now an empowered woman who could make choices that were aligned with her heart.

When we become aware of our habits and conditioning, things may seem overwhelming at first. We recognize how out of sync our behavior has been and how much we have been giving our power away. This moment of realization can be sobering and quite humbling. During our newfound awareness, we begin to see how our actions cause suffering for ourselves and those around us. This can be empowering and debilitating at the same time. Even though our reactive patterns weaken when they are pushed into our conscious awareness, it's unreasonable for us to expect them to immediately stop. We've been dancing that same dance for so long that our unconscious self knows the steps all too well.

We probably also have a lot of dance partners with whom we've been practicing the same routines for a long time, because it takes two to tango. So, when we shift, we can't expect our relationships to adapt right away either. We can stay committed to showing up in a way that feels right, and our relationships will adjust and evolve or may eventually fade away.

When our actions and attitudes are brought to the surface, we are finally able to look at them more clearly and objectively. As we become more self-aware, it's normal to experience self-judgment, but that's just another level of unconsciousness. If we can stay awake to this negative thought pattern and not indulge in that level of thinking, we begin to upgrade from being reactive to being more responsive. Seeing patterns is the first step to disrupting them.

There was a simple little trick I would use whenever I tried to bring awareness to a pattern. I would carry a little stone in my pocket throughout the day. It would remind me to be extra aware every time I reached in my pocket or felt it bounce against my leg as I walked. If I was going to have a conversation where I knew old habits were prone to come up, I would just keep my hand in my pocket and fidget with the stone. It proved to be a helpful reminder to interrupt the pattern *before* it was activated. This kind of disruption enabled me to gain dominion over my tendencies and respond to life from a more integrated and empowered perspective.

IT'S ALL ABOUT ME

I remember a time when my son was six years old, and he and his sister were fighting. After various attempts at getting him to not fight, I eventually pried him away and held on to him firmly, hoping this would make him stop. As I did, I thought to myself, "He should listen to me. He shouldn't be defiant. They shouldn't fight, and he definitely shouldn't ever hit his sister." I was completely resisting what was actually unfolding before me. As you read this, you may also be thinking, "Well, yes. A six-year-old should listen to his father, shouldn't be defiant, and shouldn't hit his sister."

The point isn't the debate of "what should or shouldn't be" but my missed opportunity to respond, rather than react, to what was happening. I was in total resistance, and thus I created suffering for both myself *and* my son. One could say my actions were legitimate or understandable, but I was approaching the problem from the wrong perspective. By holding on to my beliefs and judgments, I only made the situation worse. It was like I was adding gasoline to an already explosive situation.

I wasn't parenting effectively. Sure, I was effective in getting my son to listen to me, but only because I was controlling him physically. I effectively ended his defiance, but only because I was overpowering him. By holding him down, I stopped him from hitting his sister and was achieving what I thought I wanted. On a deeper level, it wasn't what I wanted at all. I wanted to feel connected with him. To instill a sense of respect and care for his sister. I was showing him to not use force by using force. Talk about totally missing the mark.

To put it mildly, my reaction to my son was oppressive and overpowering. I thought I could remain peaceful in almost any other situation, but there I was, completely triggered by my son's "defiance" of me and the rules of never hitting, especially a girl. By slowing things down and not turning away from what was happening, I came to realize that there may be a different way to deal with this, but it required me to let go of my position. It wasn't easy. "Of course he should listen, of course he should be respectful," my mind would argue. It was presenting me with a vivid slide show of a future where my son's life would be doomed if I allowed him to get away with his behavior. *He was six.*

By that time in my life, I was already committed to taking full responsibility for my upsets, so I had to take a hard look at my role in all of this. What I finally recognized was my younger self had been so disempowered that my son's empowerment or questioning of authority triggered me to the core. When I was my son's age, I would never have dared raise my voice, ask for explanations, or challenge my father in any way. It was as if I was saying to my son, "I didn't get to have a voice when I was young, so you won't either." As irrational and unreasonable as it was, that was my unconscious belief. It wasn't until I realized that my six-year-old self would've loved the space and ability to speak up that I was able to recognize the gift my son was actually giving me. I now had a tremendous opportunity to provide that space and celebrate his outspoken nature. This doesn't mean his behavior was justified. Not at all. But I realized the kind of kid I wanted to raise was one who could share his truth and speak up. Talk about a boomerang of understanding. It was a moment of healing. Not for my son, but for me.

Once I was able to look at my son with an open mind and without judgment, we worked together to channel his outspokenness in a more respectful and productive manner. All too often, parents who are having a hard time will focus on their children and changing their kids' behavior. While this may be important, I now believe these are those gems that provide opportunities for us to address unresolved issues within us. Children are mirrors for how we handle… everything. Acting with aggression to stop aggression only breeds aggression. When I stopped approaching him from this place, his defiance and acting out just stopped. It was fascinating to witness. It was as if, all along, he was somehow supporting me in bringing compassion to my younger self. Once I understood I had missed the experience of being able to speak my truth as a kid, I was then able to offer him that opportunity in a way that uniquely suited him. The outer shift I was looking for was a byproduct of that inner transformation. I love my boy, and I love the little boy inside of me.

An important step in this process is moving out of the attitude or perception that life is happening "to" you into one that life is happening "for" you. From this perspective, we no longer treat life as something to be overcome but rather as an ongoing invitation to liberate ourselves from the cycle of suffering. When we shift into this broader outlook, our mind remains open to the possibility of a deep trust in how things unfold. Although it hurts when your partner leaves you or you lose your job, you can still choose to be open to whatever may come next. This requires the courage to recognize the extent of our unknowing and embrace life exactly as it shows up.

Having young children in the house is a great way to shatter one's concept of perfection. As a parent, I learned the hard way that I might as well get with the program and embrace all of the ups and downs. This open embrace of the roller coaster is counterintuitive, but it makes it possible to break through the "I know better" layer that keeps us from noticing the opportunities and gifts that unfold right in front of us.

Between stimulus and response, there is a space. In that space is our power to choose our response. In our response lies our growth and our freedom.
—VIKTOR FRANKL, Austrian psychologist, Holocaust survivor

While at a concentration camp, Frankl couldn't change his external situation, so he decided to change his internal experience. If he could find freedom in the middle of a Nazi camp, we can find it anywhere. The willingness to face the undesirable in life makes it possible for us to reclaim our power. We are like that massive elephant finally ready to look at the rope around its neck as just a rope.

THE PATHLESS PATH

What I'm suggesting isn't simply a linear upgrade to a better version of our current operating system but a complete overhaul into a new way of being. Self-realization is often referred to as a path to freedom. This seems counterintuitive, since freedom only happens now, but the mind likes direction and thinks in linear terms, so we might as well call it a path.

Krishnamurti, considered by many one of the greatest spiritual teachers of the twentieth century, called this the "pathless path" because it always starts here and leads nowhere. This can be confusing to the mind, which operates exclusively in time and space. But, as Einstein suggested, we can still use the mind to take us to the edge of human understanding. At that point, we may be able to let go of our mental constructs and become willing to embrace the great unknown.

The unknown, however, is where most people turn back. Facing what's unfamiliar means we aren't able to prepare and protect, and that's very threatening to the ego. Our entire psychological structure is oriented toward safety. We can, however, reprogram our internal capacities and embody a whole new way of being. This requires an earnest curiosity, humility, and the willingness to question our assumptions by staying awake to old habits, moment to moment. The mind is where it all begins, so let's dive into it.

CHAPTER 7

MENTAL FREEDOM

As we have discussed, suffering stems from our thoughts. So, if we don't have an open mind, it is hard to shift out of the paradigm of adversity. The good news is there are some very practical tools and insights which can support us in updating our mental construct and integrating a new kind of freedom in our everyday lives.

Our challenges, whatever they might be, can be alleviated or exacerbated depending on how (or what) we are thinking about them. Something that triggers or sends you into the red line might not even register to someone else. No matter how real or difficult a situation may feel, if we suddenly give priority to something else, our focus shifts and we release the previous thought. People often say that when they go through something extremely difficult, it gives them perspective. What they are really saying is, "All those other thoughts and issues I had seem so unimportant to me now." It's as if the mind needs its container of worry filled, and it will use whichever story to fill it up. Our level of freedom can't be dependent on having things go our way, because no matter how much things go our way, there will always be something the mind can use.

One of the first steps in liberating ourselves from the whirlpool of the mind is recognizing that our thoughts are just that, thoughts. Just because we think it, doesn't make it so. Some of us are so identified with our "thinking mind," we can't distinguish between our thoughts and who we are. If we have a stupid thought, then we think we're stupid. If we think a kind thought, then we think we are kind. We give so much weight to our thinking that it becomes our identity: I am a businessman; I am a father; I am an artist, etc. When we become attached to these labels, we invest our energy in preserving them.

There are also the subtler forms of identity, like: I'm a good person; I'm hardworking; I'm honest, etc. There's nothing wrong with these qualifiers, but if we think that's all we are, then we become easily threatened: "Who am I if I'm not a [fill in the blank]?" People who take great pride in what they do, as well as who they are, often find themselves in this dilemma when circumstances change. If they lose their job, retire, lose their temper, feel lazy, become an empty nester, and so on, they can become disoriented and then scramble for another label to give their life meaning.

Sure, some thoughts can carry valuable information, but they are certainly not facts. After all, these thoughts aren't even ours, they are a byproduct of conditioning and hold very little objective truth. It's possible to be in our mind concocting a whole story and even play out conversations with different people all just inside our head. It didn't actually happen and the moment we stop thinking about the "situation," it's gone. Have you spent time strategizing about how you will handle a potential encounter only for all of it to be rendered obsolete when the incident never actually comes to fruition? You aren't alone, as it's human nature to scenarioize. Nothing wrong with fantasizing or daydreaming, but this life is a gift. Don't we actually want to be awake for it?

We simply learned to give unmerited importance to things that don't really exist in the here and now. The human mind is wonderful, but if it remains unchecked, it has the potential to wreak havoc in our psyche and create and ultimately perpetuate our suffering. The fundamental issue we tend to overlook is that the mind is an instrument and not something that defines us.

CHASING CHANGE

The mind is like a radar system, constantly synthesizing and analyzing the information our senses gather about the world and then trying to make sense out of it. This is obviously a necessary and valuable function. Like a car computer equipped with self-driving technology, the computer takes input from the road as it travels, then processes the data to assess risk. If a car computer didn't accurately reflect shifts in the external environment, however, it would no longer be functional. We haven't been updated. It's as if we're riding around in modern cars on modern highways, but parts of our mental processing mechanism remain stuck in the days of the Model T cars and unpaved roads.

The old saying that "the grass is always greener" is a perfect example of how our minds tend to work. The mind continuously scans for what's wrong or could be better in our lives. This includes just about everything we come into contact with, which can be an enormous burden. It doesn't matter how green the grass is on our side of the fence, because we have been programmed to always be on the lookout for something better.

As a species, this trait has been a critical factor and great asset in our evolution. It is the reason why we have progressed this far and why that progress continues to accelerate. While this is great, it is simply a filter we can apply to certain situations, as opposed to a permanent lens through which we must observe all of life. What makes the problem more challenging is how the mind is programmed to register the need for change and look for "what's next." This happens even when we are in a peaceful or enjoyable state of mind. When we have been happy for a short while, we begin to examine whether or not we are *really* happy. We do this because we stop feeling the shift from unhappy to happy, which is something the mind has been trained to pay attention to. We even become afraid that if we allow ourselves to be content for too long, something is bound to go wrong. A baseline of happiness is not perceived as happiness for the simple reason that it is now stabilized.

That's because happiness is perceived as the difference between a previous state and a current state, or between the current state and some future state. If the previous state was the same as the current state, it doesn't matter how happy the current state is; the mind thinks it's not enough. This process is often referred to as the hedonic adaptation. Psychologists have equated it to a treadmill where one must continually work to maintain a certain level of happiness. The mind doesn't know what to do in stable or persistent situations, except to quickly start looking for something wrong or threatening. It resists *what is*, because it thinks it knows what should be. When *what is* doesn't match what *should be,* our thoughts push back against our reality. Keeping ourselves constantly busy trying to change things prevents us from being here and enjoying where we are.

FACT CHECKING

The focus on "something better" no matter how great things are right now isn't something the mind does out of spite. It's just doing what it has been programmed to do. It is, however, possible for us to pause and create space between our thinking and the impulsive reactions that follow. This spaciousness allows us to recognize that thoughts are just thoughts and actually test their validity. Byron Katie has a process called The Work, where she invites people to release their stressful thoughts by learning how to question them. She has people ask themselves the following four questions whenever stress, and all the runaway thoughts that go with it, begin to take over:

1. Is it true?

2. Can you absolutely know it's true?

3. How do you react? What happens when you believe that thought?

4. Who would you be without that thought?

I actually used this process when I was dealing with the incident I described of attempting to control my son. This is how it went: is it true that my son should listen to me? The response in every cell of my body was, "Yes, of course, my son should listen to me. I'm his father. I have more experience than he does. I'm here to guide and support him as he tries to figure out how to navigate through life. His sister is younger than he is, and it's not OK for him to hurt her."

The second question: can you absolutely know it's true? Pondering this question, I first noticed all the reasons my mind gave for why what I was thinking should and must be true. Ultimately, however, I didn't know it was absolutely true that my son should always listen to me.

The third question: how do you react and what happens when you believe that thought?

When I put myself back in the moment of asking my son to stop roughhousing, I remember how he wasn't listening to me. In fact, he was completely ignoring me. So, when I believe the thought, "He should listen to me," I immediately become upset. Future images of him as a teenager begin to flash through my mind of him still not listening to me, getting into fights at school, or worse, hitting his girlfriend. I then imagine him as a defiant, rebellious young adult that I have a difficult time relating to. How can I help him steer clear of all the impending danger if he won't listen to me? I begin to feel the stress take hold. My heart closes a bit as I approach him and the situation with hostility and the "I know better" mindset. I fail to notice what is really happening in the moment between my son and daughter, so I jump in and intervene with physical strength to make him stop. That's what happens when I believe the thought. I'm totally caught in dysfunctional thinking and acting.

Which brings me to the fourth question: who would you be without the thought?

In that same moment, looking at my son roughhousing with his sister, without the thought that he should listen to me, I can be more curious about what is happening. I can see how hard it is for him to listen when he's in the middle of roughhousing with his sister. I've been there myself with my younger siblings when we were kids. I know what it's like to play rough. So, without the thought, I would simply be watching my son engaged in roughhousing; I'm focused on what he's actually doing, rather than what he "should" be doing. This is when I would likely notice that he wasn't really hurting his sister, because they were both involved in the tussle; she's actually quite the powerhouse. I further realize the manufactured urgency I'm approaching the situation with because I believed the thought of "this needs to stop immediately!"

It wasn't a life-or-death situation, as my mind wanted me to believe. My heart could now open to both my son *and* my daughter as well as the situation as a whole. Without believing the thought, I could now approach what was happening with a much more creative attitude and open perceptiveness. In the end, I could meet my kids where they were in their moment of wildness. I could meet my son where he was by seeing how much fun they were having together. I had the entire situation backward. I was overbearing because, again, I was under the impression that I knew better.

From a psychological perspective, the recognition of what was happening and the deeper opportunity behind the seeming chaos of my kids roughhousing was a big one for me. I was grateful that this awareness enabled me to stop my behavior and judgments of the situation and helped me break the generational pattern I was playing out. I shifted from resistance to acceptance—not a condoning of my children hitting each other, but the capacity to recognize when a reactive pattern gets in the way of allowing them to be children at play.

Shifts like these have made me a better parent: Better at fostering healthy relationships with my children. Better at recognizing the opportunities to integrate disenfranchised aspects within me. And better at consciously exploring what kind of dad I want to be. My old operating system had been running on conditioned autopilot to control my surroundings and protect my identity as a dad who raises kids who listen. These instructions simply needed to be reprogrammed and updated.

A few days later, when my kids were at it again, I was ready for it. Instead of trying to control the situation, my new "software" kicked in and I just observed them. In the midst of their wrestling, my son noticed I wasn't trying to stop him. I could see he was working things out on his own. It was as if he was trying to understand how and why this situation was different. Perhaps it had something to do with the observer effect. In physics, the observer effect is the theory that the mere observation of a phenomenon will inevitably change the phenomenon. I watched how my son became aware of his actions, almost saying to himself, "Maybe I shouldn't play so rough." He continued to play, but he was way gentler, and I didn't have to say a word.

For me, I could see that my son wasn't actually hurting his sister. If he did, my daughter would signal with a cry for help, and I would certainly act differently. But I could now see their "roughhousing" was, again, two children at play. The matrix of my conditioning had been cleared and I finally saw them in their element—children, being children.

Over time, my son and I have forged a relationship of mutual respect. He still wrestles with his sister and is very much a bull in a china shop at times, but he now knows his voice matters. For me, I knew I would no longer try to overpower or intimidate him into cooperation or try to control him. Now, this doesn't mean my son and daughter don't fight. I understand it's part of the sibling DNA, but I did notice a shift. Something was different. My son was different. I was different. How I handled the situation was different. My choice actually provided the space for him to take responsibility for his actions.

Now, whenever things get out of control, or chaos grabs hold of a situation, my son and I are able talk about it. It enables both of us to see how we might have contributed to the chaos or what role we might have played therein. He's no longer invested in defending his innocence, because he knows we're on the same team in this game of figuring out what works and what doesn't. For my son. For myself. For everyone involved.

When we are out of sync, frustrated, or stuck, our energy affects everything around us. When we are able to move past judgmental thoughts, we are more authentic and centered. For me, I am more present as a father when I am not in judgment. From there, I can empower and encourage their autonomy as young people.

By observing my thoughts like a pedestrian crossing the street, I can also watch them walk away. No need to engage with them. When the old thoughts or judgments come up and I don't believe them, they tend to just move on. I am more able to see my children as they are and not as an idea of how they *should* be. Despite my best efforts, my children can tell how much I am in acceptance or judgment of them at any given moment, and I've come to see that as a good thing. I love my kids with everything I am. Through them, I have been able to see and feel love like never before. They also continue to point out all those areas within me that still need tending to. For that, I am eternally grateful.

SLAYING "SHOULD"

The degree to which we are able to have an open mind affects how we show up in life. A closed mind is filled with *shoulds*. "My kids *should* listen to me. I *should* be on time for this very important meeting. My partner *should* be more considerate. My employees *should* know what to do. I *should* be thinner. My boss *should* be nicer."

I'm not suggesting anyone stay in a harmful relationship or in a job that isn't serving their highest expression, but in order for us to change, we don't need to resist what is happening. We are much better at discernment from a place of acceptance. What happened, happened. Always. If a vendor delivered late, that's merely information. All the stories that spin out from a fact only create suffering. That suffering gives me far less room to see or hear creative solutions to any given situation. By lowering my resistance to what is happening in my work life, I am able to show up for my employees and vendors and make appropriate adjustments. I can have a conversation with a supplier to set clear expectations. If those expectations aren't met, I am able to take action. I don't need to judge vendors if I need to replace them. That's the difference between resistance and discernment.

It is easy to make decisions when we have a clear yes or even a clear no. The struggle is when things aren't so cut and dry. This is when we need the space to evaluate situations effectively. But we can't really do that when we operate from a place of judgment.

When one of my children is having a hard time with a decision, I invite them to envision a balance scale. The arguments in favor and against their potential choices are like weights tipping the balance to one side or the other. Some things weigh more than others, but "shoulds" and "shouldn'ts" are among the heaviest. In order for them to be able to notice the lighter weights, such as their inner guidance and intuition, those heavy loads need to be placed to the side. I invite them to identify all the ideas of what's "supposed to happen" and then to suspend them for a moment. "Without all the shoulds and shouldn'ts, what feels right?"

That space also allows us to recognize when we don't know. Not knowing or seeing a possible solution is OK. The mind isn't comfortable with uncertainty, though. When faced with "not knowing," it can spin off into a cycle of doubt. If we find ourselves in doubt, we are basically saying, "I don't know... yet." We suffer when we think, "I *should* know." The thing we need to remember, especially as a parent or entrepreneur, is that there is nothing wrong with not having clarity all the time. Sometimes we can see the matrix clearly and sometimes it's like walking around with a blanket over our heads. And that's OK, because that's part of any journey. When faced with lack of clarity, sometimes doing nothing is the best course of action. Unfortunately, however, this isn't something that is widely taught in our homes, classrooms, or workplaces. When we aren't in resistance to not yet knowing, suffering doesn't rear its ugly head, and odds are in our favor that we'll be in a better mental space to discover the clarity we desire.

There's another framework that's been valuable to me, my children, and my mentees, which entails observing areas of our lives where we find ourselves dealing with doubt or uncertainty. It's like a decision gradient with three distinct color zones: white (yes), black (no), and gray (everything in between). In life, there are decisions that are black or white. At this point in my life, stealing is black. I don't really need to decide whether or not I'm going to take something that doesn't belong to me. Telling you I just saw your cards while playing poker is white, because it's not something I need to consider; I'm going to tell you. There are a lot of other issues that fall more into the gray zone.

At one point, I felt I didn't want to be in business with someone because I didn't enjoy his personality. I often found myself complaining about how he showed up in our business relationship. With regards to this partnership, I had one foot in and one foot out. It wasn't a full yes, but it wasn't a clear no, either, because the business opportunity was compelling to me. This is when I realized there was a direct correlation between the size of the gray zone in a particular area of my life and how at peace I felt. The more gray there was, the more uncomfortable I became. I decided to make a commitment to look at all the gray areas in my life and close the gap by turning them, whenever possible, into a black or a white decision.

When I couldn't come to a full yes or no, which only meant I didn't have enough clarity, I decided to move forward only if and when I arrived at a full "yes." In the case of this partner, I moved out of the gray zone and into the white. When I stopped complaining, I began to recognize even with his personality traits, I still wanted to be in the business relationship. Interestingly enough, the things that once bothered me about my partner either stopped happening or stopped bothering me altogether. I further recognized how the gray zone kept me on the lookout for what wasn't working, which is a toxic and disempowering place to be.

COMPARISON AND CRITICISM

If suffering is a self-inflicted and optional state of being, why do we continue to choose it? The mind is convinced its main role is to be the story's protagonist or the control tower that oversees everything. One of the mind's most harmful, yet preferred, methods for exerting its agenda is self-judgment. It is convinced that if it doesn't judge and criticize, nothing will ever change. We therefore dwell on all the ways we come up short of our expectations and use comparison as the weapon to inflict pain with thoughts like: "I should look different than I do. I'm a bad father. She's more successful than I am. I can never stick with a diet."

Our mind isn't trying to hurt us; it's just that self-criticism is the default mode of course correction. It sees us as its self-improvement project and does its very best to convince us we're not good enough as we are. From its own perspective, the mind believes it is fulfilling a clearly defined and necessary purpose for our benefit. However, rather than helping us to evolve, these thoughts can be quite paralyzing. Making us feel guilty is our operating system's outdated means to get results, but the truth is that we can learn, adapt, and grow without the hurtful judgment.

This can be a tricky pattern to break free from. It's easy to become addicted to our victimhood, guilt, and self-punishment. The closed mind (the ego) is comfortable in its ways. In order for change to take place, we need to be willing to explore a different approach. There's an experiment you can conduct to understand the reasoning behind these judgments. The next time you have a stressful thought, see if you can explore what's underneath. What is the intention behind this thought? How is it trying to be helpful? What is it really saying?

Let's look at the following example: "I shouldn't have stayed up last night binging Netflix." The underlying purpose of that thought may be to remind us that we value sleeping. That reminder may still be relevant, but there are much more efficient and effective ways of supporting us in modifying our behavior that don't involve negativity. Unconsciously, we believe we deserve to be judged. Meaning, if we don't criticize our behavior, we'll never change. Growing up, we probably learned to associate punishment and feeling guilt or shame for doing something "bad," so now we do it to ourselves. We can, however, recognize the value of the underlying intention within the criticism and find more self-honoring ways of holding ourselves accountable.

VANESSA

Not too long after giving birth, my friend Vanessa was having a difficult time. During her pregnancy, she had gained more weight than she wanted to and was struggling to get back in shape. At first, it was hard for her to recognize that the feeling of guilt and self-defeating thoughts like, "I shouldn't have eaten that dessert," weren't helping her situation. She thought that if it she didn't criticize her behavior, she wouldn't course correct. Eventually, Vanessa was willing to consider the possibility that change could happen without the punishing voices. She recognized that, as harsh as it was, the underlying intention of her inner critic was to support her in getting back in shape and eating a healthier diet. When I invited her to go deeper, she discovered eating a healthier diet translated into a more deep-seated intention: self-acceptance. It was shocking for her to recognize the critic's underlying intent was getting her to accept herself more fully. The way in which it was helping her currently, however, was creating the opposite effect.

The self-critic can be our greatest ally, if we can update the way it's trying to help. Vanessa was able to shift her relationship with this inner voice and acknowledge it for actually trying to support her. She then enrolled this very diligent aspect in an experiment. Instead of attacking her with judgments, it would act as a reminder to practice self-acceptance. This ever-present, always vigilant voice inside of her could be used as an asset to help her love herself more fully, independent of her weight. She bypassed the superficial target of being thin and was able to go directly to fulfilling the underlying purpose of having self-esteem.

She chose a different part of her body to appreciate per week and repatterned the way she saw herself. For the first time in her life, Vanessa was not on a diet and, to her surprise, gradually shifted toward healthier eating habits. It's as if in the absence of the self-critic vigilante, the unhealthy habits no longer had a reason to be. Fixations stay in place because there's an action and reaction. When we drop the judgment, the action loses momentum.

Going through self-judgment as a way of getting to self-acceptance seems like a counterintuitive process. It is, but since we have been doing it for such a long time, it's irrational to expect it to change right away. We can instead approach this new strategy like a scientist, curiously testing it out.

I'm addicted to checking my phone. I became aware of this bad habit and knew something needed to change. Even when I know I checked my phone only a few minutes ago, I still pull it out and check to see if I missed anything or if anything new has come in. It's one thing if I am waiting for an important email, but 99.9 percent of the time, I'm not. Giving into the impulse and expecting to find some urgent message that wasn't there a few minutes ago is pretty unconscious behavior. The second the phone is open, the scrolling begins. I check mail. I check the news. I glance at the stock ticker. I check, check, and check again. Now that I have become aware of the habit, I have learned to take a conscious breath before picking up my phone. Through breathing and taking a momentary beat, I can then deliberately decide if I'll act on the impulse or wait. This way, I'm not judging the impulse itself but bringing awareness and space to a formerly unconscious action. Most of the time, I realize it's completely unnecessary to check it right that very second. Other times, I opt in and go for it. As my youngest daughter always says, "If you do it, don't judge it...if you judge it, don't do it."

IT'S NOT YOU...IT'S ME

In psychology, the term "projection" is the premise that what we see and judge in others simply reflects something we see and judge in ourselves. At first, this concept can be hard to embrace, as it means whatever triggers us is ours to deal with. The external event is just pointing to something we haven't made peace with internally.

Some projections can be quite obvious, because we know we do the exact thing we are choosing to judge others of doing. Other projections, however, can be far more subtle. We may even judge a behavior in others that we are either capable of doing, given the right circumstances, or wish we could do but know we would feel guilty about.

Whenever I find myself slipping into a judgment of others, I ask myself a powerful question: "If I were in that person's exact same life circumstances—upbringing, limitations, and frame of mind—can I be absolutely sure I wouldn't be doing the very thing I am judging them for?"

You never really understand a person until you
consider things from his point of view...
until you climb inside of his skin and walk around in it.
—ATTICUS FINCH, Character in *To Kill a Mockingbird*

Recognizing that we're all capable of committing what we would deem unacceptable, given the right conditions, can free us from both our judgments of the other person and ourselves.

Judgment is everywhere in our society. Commenting is just what our minds do; how we relate to that commentary is where the opportunity lies. A common example of all this is road rage. Living here in Southern California, I have witnessed some gnarly behavior on our crowded freeways. It seems so irrational that people would go into a knee-jerk, judgmental rant about someone who just cut them off and, thereby, take it as a personal, inexcusable offense. However, with a moment of consideration, we all realize at some point in our lives as drivers we've done something similar, if not worse.

The more we can look at life as the mirror that it is, the more we become empowered to look at the places inside ourselves that need additional attention. Taking responsibility for our projections shines light into the dark corners of our being where the things we really don't approve of hide. In order for true freedom to flourish, these hidden aspects need to be met with compassion, forgiveness, and self-acceptance.

Sometimes a projection is evident and sometimes we need to look a little closer. Such was the case when I encountered a woman selling her body for money. Upon seeing her, I immediately went into judgment and started thinking of all the other, more creative ways she might have been able to provide for herself. "Of course, this isn't a projection," I thought to myself. "I would never do such a thing if I were in that position. I would be able to find a million other ways to make a living."

I then began to explore what might be called the "prostitute archetype." I dug a little deeper and realized I viewed the prostitute as someone who exchanged integrity for money. Integrity can be defined as the honesty and truthfulness or accuracy of one's actions. I was saying, "It's wrong to compromise your principles in exchange for money." Now, that was something I was definitely familiar with. I knew I had compromised my values in exchange for things and ignored what felt *right* for me multiple times. I remembered all the instances when I had tried to fit in while doing business by agreeing with someone's opinion, even though I had actually held a completely different point of view. There were also numerous times I had drunk alcohol at business dinners even though I hadn't wanted to and laughed at jokes I hadn't found funny in order to belong and cultivate a comfortable environment focused on potentially closing a deal.

I realized I was justifying my actions, even though they weren't aligned with my truth. I didn't even know if the sex worker was out of integrity; I didn't know her truth. Once I owned up to this idea within myself, I could forgive and release the judgment I had for all the ways I had "prostituted" myself. I was also able to recognize how I couldn't be sure I wouldn't sell my body for money if I had the same upbringing and challenges as the woman I was judging. Let me be clear: releasing judgment does not imply that you agree with others' actions or believe that what they or you do is without consequences. There is a distinction between judging and our capacity to discern or evaluate any given situation. I may disapprove of a behavior in someone else, but I don't need to sit in judgment to speak up for what I believe to be right or just. Sure, I may have strong preferences for how I want people to treat me, but I don't need to be judgmental to set clear boundaries.

One interesting exercise is to write down the name of someone you judge strongly, adding your complaints about them. Write down, "Francis is a [blank]," and fill in the blank with each and every judgment about Francis that comes up for you. When that is finished, do a virtually identical list in which you substitute "I am" for "Francis is." Look at all the ways in which you are or do what you have projected onto Francis. The mind will dart around this exercise, because it requires you to drop any positionality against Francis. Some judgments may be less apparent, like the case with prostitution was for me. But, if you are able to sit with them long enough, you will find examples of how every external condemnation is reflecting an internal one.

Realizing that everyone and everything we judge is essentially highlighting parts of us needing attention requires enormous courage and humility. But letting go of self-righteousness allows us to find a doorway to our own healing and transformation. Perhaps the next time you see or think about Francis, a bit more spaciousness will open up in your mind (and heart) around her and what she is going through.

Taking this level of responsibility gives us an opportunity to look at people and situations more clearly. It's both liberating and efficient to recognize that we don't need to judge in order to discern and act appropriately. If, for instance, we are in an abusive relationship, we don't need to blame, shame, or criticize our partner in order move away from the relationship. All we have to do is get clear with what is right and appropriate for us. By releasing the attachment to our habits and our stories, we are able to take effective action that is in alignment with our values. When someone breaks the law, we send them to prison. Their behavior or lack of respect for the law has a way of wearing away the social fabric of society, but we don't need to sustain a grudge for them personally. If we do, animosity and resentment become the self-imposed verdict that only ends up imprisoning us. This is a much different way of administering a criminal justice system than acting from the unresolved places within ourselves. Prison's purpose would then truly be focused on the behavior and the possibility for rehabilitation, rather than the punishment, of the individual.

In some Eastern cultures, as well as in some African tribes, people who commit crimes are spoken of as having caught a virus that needs healing. This distinguishes individuals from their criminal actions. The individuals are not condemned personally. Their actions are, and the community focuses on ways to support these people in realigning themselves back into society or the tribe, as it were.

WARPED PERCEPTION

Our mind filters what we sense and perceive through our conditioning, assumptions, and preconceptions. When we observe things, we come up with our own personalized set of conclusions about them. Judging or admiring someone or something actually says a lot more about our filters than it says about the other person or situation we are focused on. This is why a hundred people can witness the same event and see it a hundred different ways. By perceiving life from our "wounding," it's like we are in the carnival mirror from *Alice in Wonderland*, bending and distorting everything around us. The more unresolved wounds we have, the more warped our vision appears.

Our filters are ultimately imposing their own, distorted sense of reality on top of what is actually going on. This distortion field informs our notions of how things "should be" and uses resistance as a mechanism to correct what's being reflected, rather than addressing the wounds or cracks in the reflecting mirror itself. That is why intimate relationships, romantic or otherwise, can appear to be so challenging. The closer people get to one another, the more distorted the reflection becomes. Once someone gets close enough, it is compelling to move on and find something that's a little further out. This gives rise to phenomena like serial dating. Images will always be changing, so unless the mirror is addressed, our perception will keep being hazy. If we stop ignoring our wounds and avoiding what triggers us, we can use what comes up as a way to repair the underlying distortion. Let's explore ways to do this by using our emotions as a roadmap in this process of restoration.

CHAPTER 8

EMOTIONAL FREEDOM

I used to think emotional freedom meant not experiencing or feeling "bad" emotions. I believed if I was feeling good, I was succeeding. If I was sad, however, then something was wrong and needed fixing. My identity as a happy person was so important that I did whatever necessary to sustain that happy feeling. I was very attentive to how I spent my time and intent on being with people who uplifted me and helped me feel better about myself.

It seemed reasonable to put myself in situations or experiences that elevated me, but this selective way of living was very disempowering. I became dependent on life showing up in a certain way and on my perceived capacity to avoid the negative and attract the positive. Misguided, sure. Reasonable? Maybe. Sustainable? Not so much. There were times when one thing would really bother me, and other times when it wouldn't. The only thing different was my story about what was going on. My emotions had less to do with the given situation and more to do with my interpretation of what was happening.

Emotions are neither good nor bad in and of themselves. They are the manifestations of how our body responds to the stories we tell. Feelings follow thoughts, which means our thinking is really at the root of all of our emotions. Even though they often seem to occur all on their own, an interpretation is required for emotional feelings to arrive in the body. All this happens very quickly, particularly with deep-rooted beliefs, but if you become curious enough to examine the arising emotion, you can uncover the perception that triggered the sensation.

IT'S JUST ENERGY

Here in the West, a lot of us have become proficient at coping with emotions by not expressing them in public and sometimes not even in private settings. We are taught "positive" emotions like excitement are good, but "negative" emotions like sadness, fear, and anger are "bad." Parents often tell their children, in so many words, the purpose of life is to be happy. The implication is that if your life isn't happy at any given moment, something is wrong.

When we closely examine our emotions, however, we realize they are just energy. Where we get into trouble is when we assign that energy a positive or negative charge through our interpretation or perception of it. When my children are afraid of something, I invite them to become curious about what they are feeling. Children have had less time than adults to develop coping mechanisms, so they often have an easier time removing the labels from sensations. Simply put, children have less practice at avoiding.

During a recent trip to Mount Shasta in Northern California, my children wanted to jump off a bridge into the lake below. When we made our way to the bridge, they were hanging on to the rail for dear life. I must admit, my wife and I were also holding on pretty tight, because it was higher than it had seemed from below. We all really wanted to jump but were also terrified at the same time. We got curious of those coexisting emotions and explored what they actually felt like in the body. My daughter was first to point out that the experience of fear was very similar to the experience of excitement. The underlying energy actually felt identical in both cases, and for all of us, it was expressed as a stirring in the pit of our stomachs. What distinguishes the two emotions is the accompanying thought, which projects itself into the future. When we're afraid, we think, "If I jump off this cliff, I could die." When we're excited, we could be imagining the exhilarating experience of free fall to the water below.

It can be quite invigorating to experience that raw energy. However, trying to avoid, manage, or control it can be depleting. "I've got to get over being afraid! Look at her, she jumped! She's so much braver than I am! I should be able to do the same!" When we do this, we are coping with the natural energetic sensation by shifting into our analytical mind. Everyone uses different mechanisms to "not feel" certain things in life, but resisting emotions is like attempting to hold an inflated ball under water. No matter how much we want the ball to stay down, it will continue to push to the surface. Trying to keep our emotions submerged in the background of our experience is an exhausting, full-time job.

When we're out of sync with or unaccustomed to facing our emotional world, we become disconcerted when the emotions eventually rise to the surface. This is when our accumulated baggage suddenly "comes out of nowhere." Human beings are expressive by nature, and emotions become blocked energy when not allowed to naturally flow. If bottled up, the emotions are lodged somewhere in our body, but ultimately they will find another way to express themselves.

My youngest daughter has taught me a lot about this. When she experiences deep sadness or hurt, she is able to come right out of it. I call this ability her "emotional cycle," which remains free and fluid. I remember trying to make her feel better when she was sad, not realizing that I was projecting my own issues onto her. I was essentially saying, "Your sadness is not OK with me." Luckily, she didn't comply, and I paid attention and actually learned from her process. If we are attentive enough, children can model so much for us.

TEMPORARY AND SHORT-LIVED

My experience is that emotions are short-lived if they are experienced without being bolstered or justified by a recurring story. As demonstrated by my daughter, without the additional narrative, emotions such as sadness, anger, and even joy tend to appear in and move through her body rather quickly. According to Dr. Jill Bolte Taylor, a Harvard-trained and published neuroscientist, "When a person has a reaction to something in their environment, there's a 90-second chemical process that happens in the body; after that, any remaining emotional response is just the person choosing to stay in that emotional loop." I've never counted exactly, but that observation matches my own experience.

One of the ways I've worked with both my children and the people I mentor around their emotions is to help them get intimate with the sensation. First, we identify and sense its location in our body. Once located, we can approach what's actually going on with curiosity, being mindful of the tendency to label the feeling. This neutral observation counteracts the impulse to resist what's happening and allows the emotion to exist. The more intimate I am able to become with an emotion, the less uncomfortable it actually feels. Discomfort is a function of resistance rather than a direct experience *of* the emotion itself. This short process quickly reduces the intensity of what felt like an overwhelming sensation simply because we consciously allowed it to be. Trying to counteract emotions is like being on a boat in the ocean, trying to prevent the waves from swaying you back and forth. The more you let go and settle into the rhythm, the more enjoyable the boat ride will be.

MOVING THE ENERGY

Most people don't distinguish between emotions and actions, even though feelings and behaviors are completely different. Feeling an emotion is part of being alive; it's the acting out of those emotions that needs to be carried out in a respectful manner, if it is to be sustainable. Because I never learned to differentiate between them, I used to associate anger with aggression and sadness with isolation. I judged aggression as being wrong, so I ultimately found anger unacceptable. When something upset me, I would go straight to feeling victimized, as this seemed more socially acceptable. I learned to be passive aggressive, to close down and blame, as a covert way to hit back at whatever was going on in my life.

When my kids are angry, I recommend they find the capacity to be with the anger and move that energy in a healthy manner. There are appropriate places and respectful ways to express our emotions. If we allow the raw sensations to exist, the energy itself can find its natural flow. Sometimes, however, we dig in and become invested in holding on to an emotion, because there are parts of us that aren't ready to let go. Therein lies the work. Thanks to my children, I have relearned how to relate with emotions and be curious when they arrive. This can be a tall order, but I try to honor the feelings and, when appropriate, examine any unresolved issues that may be at their root. Sometimes, recurring emotions are like nudges from the subconscious, signaling that we are in need of healing.

DREW

To illustrate this, I want to share about a friend we'll refer to as "Drew." Drew and his older brother were partners in a real estate business. He loved his brother but would constantly feel triggered by him. Drew was often angry and had been considering selling his share of the business because he felt attacked and patronized. Drew would often say to himself, "If I don't act angry, my brother won't know how serious this is for me. He put me down in front of my colleagues and that's not OK. If he sees me not reacting, then he'll only do it again."

Since I knew this wasn't the first time Drew and his brother had had problems, I prodded, "How is the strategy of being aggressive working for you?" Drew acknowledged it didn't do any good when he held on to his anger. Nothing would really change. The pattern was Drew would get mad and his brother would get defensive. After some time, as most siblings can, they would move on, but every one of these bouts would chip away at Drew's excitement for the business.

Because he loved his brother and he cared about the business, Drew was open enough to explore a new way to navigate this dynamic. Before this moment, he was convinced if he didn't act mad, his brother would just dismiss the situation as nonsense and keep doing it. He knew it was a risk to do something different, because it made him feel vulnerable, but he was willing. By acknowledging his anger independent of his need to act it out, he was able to get in touch with experiencing a deep hurt. He knew there was pain there, but he hadn't actually connected with it because he would immediately cover it with the louder sensation of upset. He was able to use the exercise we talked about earlier and question the thought, "I need to be mad in order for him to change." Once he saw his upset was not necessary, he felt less contracted around the situation and decided to write a letter to his brother.

Drew began his letter by telling his brother how much he loved him. He spent the next two paragraphs recalling memories they shared as kids and some of their adventures growing up. He illustrated how they were always looking out for each other. These momentary reflections of his love for his brother and the time they shared together resulted in a healing revelation for Drew. By putting his thoughts down on paper, leading with love first, Drew realized his brother wasn't the only person he felt patronized by. As is the case with most issues, they tend to show up across different areas of our lives. Remember, upsets are wounds getting activated by projecting hurt and looking for resolution, anywhere. He wasn't sure he would give his brother the letter, but he was no longer feeling so antagonistic toward him.

He later told me he decided against sending the letter. He did, however, have a sincere conversation with his brother from this new place of clarity. Drew taking responsibility and acknowledging this was his issue to work through made the conversation a lot more productive. He could still give his brother feedback, set clear boundaries, and request a change in behavior, but he was no longer blaming and feeling victimized. This enabled him to take better care of himself without holding on to resentment. Sharing his experience of the situation without wronging his brother kept his brother's defenses from coming up, which created enough room for Drew to be heard.

I often encourage my children and mentees to explore different ways of letting energy circulate through their bodies. Since we are so trained to manage our experiences, most people find it valuable to have a recurring practice so they can process emotional energy more consciously. Some prefer to channel their emotions through writing, while others may go on a run or put on some boxing gloves. My oldest daughter likes to "dance it out." She also chooses to do things like go for a walk, breathe, and take some personal space to journal. My son likes to lightly rub his nose with three fingers as if he was somehow helping the energy go up. We all have our own special way of navigating things; what's important is to have the ability to call ourselves back from an emotional rabbit hole.

Have you ever noticed how animals shake their bodies or make wild noises after a hostile encounter? They literally shake off the energy and go about their business. In his book, *The Power of Now*, renowned spiritual teacher and bestselling author, Eckhart Tolle, talks about this and how ducks will separate after a fight, flap their wings a few times to release the built-up energy, and move on. They don't have a human mind, so they don't seem to hold on to a story that perpetuates further emotional distress or chaos. I'm holding out for a world where it would be seen as normal for a guy to be at a family gathering and, instead of closing down or attacking after feeling triggered, suddenly flap his arms and "shake it off."

EMOTION IN BUSINESS

When we enter the business world, vulnerability and emotions have a tendency to become suppressed and even prohibited. Feelings are often said to get in the way of the work. I tend to disagree. Entrepreneurs have a way of hiding their insecurities under the rug, especially with investors. Whenever I invest in a start-up, I am choosing to invest in the people as much as the business model. I try and give the entrepreneur permission to be emotionally available as much as they are invested in what they are doing. It takes them a minute to trust that it's OK to open up, because they are so trained to promote their businesses by appearing confident to everyone.

Inviting them to admit they don't have it all together can actually liberate them from having to manage and hide their apprehensions. Ultimately, this makes them better entrepreneurs because they are empowered to express their concerns and ask for help. With this open line of communication, I am able to be a better resource for them. I need to know the entrepreneurs I invest in are aware enough to recognize weaknesses within their companies and themselves. This doesn't diminish my trust in them. Quite the contrary: an entrepreneur who is in touch with the emotional body and all its subtleties and cues is much better suited to navigate the nuances of any venture.

When I speak of allowing emotions to exist, I'm not suggesting we indulge in them, which is just the opposite side of denying them. Emotional mastery is the capacity to feel the feelings, take the feedback they're providing, and then let them move through. Entrepreneurs and businesspeople alike often seem to think they need to hold on to their upsets—for example, the anger they have for a colleague who "wronged" them or a competitor who poached an employee or launched a product line similar to theirs. They may think their competitor has done something underhanded and disgraceful and that letting go of the anger equals letting them off the hook. As we saw with Drew, they don't need the anger to take appropriate action. If they hold on to this anger, however, they start operating out of a narrow outlook solely focused on beating someone or showing why they or their products are better. There's nothing wrong with competition or competitive energy, but it is inefficient when that competitive drive relies on upset as fuel because it compromises the creative impulse.

When I invite entrepreneurs to get in touch with their upsets, they usually vent for a bit and then feel drained. This exhaustion finally allows them to realize they feel hurt and sad, because they authentically care about what they are doing. When I can support angry entrepreneurs in connecting with their underlying care for their companies, their employees, their shareholders, and the community, a whole new love for what they're creating can become unlocked. They get a boost of energy to do their best work.

While antagonism is narrow, care is open, creative, and full of potential. If an entrepreneur hasn't been allowed to become comfortable with their emotions, these emotions could become the background noise behind everything they do. When they are upset, they become invested in staying upset. They stay irritated because they think if they move on, they'll become overly permissive. They almost believe it's their responsibility to stay "in it," because if they didn't, they would be excusing whatever they feel is wrong. However, that's not at all what they're doing when they hang on to an emotion. The person hurt most by this is themselves.

By extension, whatever they choose to engage in ultimately carries that undertone.

Feelings are meant to be experienced and released, not carried around as reminders or weapons for future use. When people can distinguish between forgiving and condoning, they can liberate a lot of the energetic baggage and still take appropriate action. Forgiving someone (or yourself) is recognizing they did the best they could do given their capacities and limitations at the time. Again, this does not mean you can't do what needs to be done, but you don't need to hold on to anger in order to choose a different path or set clear expectations.

THE BOARD OF DIRECTORS

One technique I find particularly helpful is to ask individuals to explore all the different aspects within themselves and treat them like members of a company's board of directors. Each one of these internal board members is given a name and assigned a specific role. The board member who judges them when they eat a muffin might be known as "Healthy Dude." The board member who tells them they should be further up the corporate ladder could be the "Career Guy." The Career Guy, the Healthy Dude, the Planner, the Social One: all these characters take turns being the predominant voice in our heads. Their opinions often arrive in quick succession, like: "I shouldn't eat that muffin. Eat it. Life is meant to be enjoyed. You never stick to your diets anyway. I can't believe I ate that muffin. I've got to go to the gym tomorrow."

From a business perspective, this is a disjointed and ineffective way of running a company. If you ignore any of your board members, however, all you are doing is forcing them to speak even louder and send memos in the form of more mental noise. To run the business of our lives effectively, we have to make room for our board members to be heard, so they can not only coexist but begin to work in harmony.

On the surface, their agendas may seem to be different. One board member may want you to be adventurous and just go out and enjoy life. Another might want you to work hard to attain financial independence. A third may want you to prioritize self-improvement. When these apparent agendas aren't brought together in the board room, we generally wind up bouncing from one to another. However, when we look at their ultimate purpose, there is usually commonality and an overlapping intention.

At their core, all of our board members want to benefit the company, which, in this case, means you. When we get underneath their superficial posturing, we allow all these aspects of ourselves to recognize they are aligned and actually share the same purpose. From that unanimity, it's a lot easier to arrive at a cohesive strategy that incorporates all their feedback and perspectives.

I've seen the board member exercise help people make enormous shifts in both their personal and professional lives. The amount of energy spent trying to manage all the different voices when they pull us in different directions can be exhausting. When managed correctly by honoring and valuing their unique perspectives, a powerful alignment can occur.

SAM

From one adventure to the next, my friend "Sam" spent most of his twenties traveling the world. As he approached his thirties, Sam realized he needed to make a steady living so he could buy a home one day. He dug in and started working hard to make this happen. Unexpectedly, he found himself in a serious relationship with a girl and began to contemplate the idea of one day asking her to marry him.

With all this going on, he found himself being tugged in many different directions by his inner voices, the board members. Sam and I did an exercise where he invited all these different parts of himself to have a turn at the microphone. It was fascinating to watch because he really went for it. He got into character representing the various perspectives and his voice and body posture even matched the various roles. The Adventurer board member enthusiastically said, "Let's just go and play. Let's travel." The Work Hard board member seriously and with a deeper voice responded, "No, no, no, no, no. You've got to work eighty hours a week; we need to have enough savings before we can just take off."

The Adventurer wanted nothing to do with postponing Sam's happiness. Its attitude was, "Might as well just enjoy life right now." When it looked at Sam's budding romantic relationship, the voice thought, "Wait. Will I lose my freedom if I have children?" These parts all seemed to be representing different agendas and were certainly causing confusion and suffering for Sam. In the end, however, Sam discovered all of his voices were actually looking for the same thing.

It was shocking for Sam to discover that his entire board was motivated by the wish for him to be happy and enjoy life. Even the Work Hard board member admitted that he was really saying, "Work hard so that you can enjoy life." Perceiving his board members' deepest interests were aligned, Sam got clear that their overall intention was to support him in fulfilling his purpose: to live his life full-out by holding back nothing.

We talked earlier about "finding your purpose" and how I encourage people to connect their overarching purpose with how they're showing up, moment to moment. What qualities will they express when living this purpose? Nothing stays the same, so purpose must be subject to constant self-inquiry. Sam's purpose turned out to be live life fully, or, as he put it, "to be all in." Whether he was working twelve-hour days or traveling for fun, whether he was single or married and a father, his "to be all in" purpose could always be fulfilled.

He was no longer outsourcing his fulfillment to external events and circumstances. This perspective allowed Sam to bring all the different parts of himself (his board members) and turn these many voices into something of a cheering chorus. It didn't matter if he was stuck at an airport because of a delayed flight, if he was cliff diving, or if he was in a hospital because his wife was about to go into labor. Sam finally realized he could live his purpose, no matter what his situation might be.

WORKING THROUGH FEAR

The technique of dialoguing with our different, often conflicting, parts derives from Gestalt therapy. Developed by Fritz Perls, Laura Perls, and Paul Goodman in the 1940s, Gestalt therapy is a client-centered approach to psychotherapy which helps clients focus on the present and understand what is really happening in their lives *right now*, rather than what they may perceive to be happening based on their past experiences. One way of using Gestalt therapy is by surfacing and giving voice to the various aspects that operate in our psyche and uncover their motivations and fears.

Sam's Work Hard board member told him he should forget his desire to travel and just work as hard as he could. A Gestalt dialogue would ask the Work Hard voice, "What are you afraid would happen to Sam if you weren't around to give him advice, or if he didn't listen to you?" The response from Work Hard might be, "Well, Sam would be flying all over the world doing nothing." The dialogue would then continue, "What if Sam were flying all over the world doing nothing? Then what?" This aspect might respond, "At some point, he would run out of money and he would end up broke."

The process of inquiry keeps drilling down even further: "What would happen if Sam ran out of money? He would be homeless and unhappy. Then what?" A pause might follow, which is the kind of pause that could give a new insight a chance to emerge. "Well, he would need to find a new way to earn money to live on." At this turning point, the dialogue can start to take a different, more fruitful direction. "Sam might move back to the ranch where he grew up herding cattle. Actually, that wouldn't be so bad, would it? He might actually be quite happy doing that. Or maybe he could move to a small town and become a teacher, as he thought he might be when he was younger." The point was for Sam to explore, confront, and hold a dialogue with the fear that was holding him down, rather than continuing to suppress it or resist it. This brings a vague and intangible concern down to earth and examines it rigorously.

Fear thrives in ambiguity. Freedom or liberation results from being able to look at fear closely enough in order to see all the way through it. This is not about silencing valid concerns but piercing through superficial worries, such as not making more money, and connecting with deeper considerations, such as "being happy." Once fear is encountered and examined closely, its concerns can be taken into consideration, while keeping overall well-being in mind.

Sam now knew how to harmonize the various board members to live "on purpose" wherever he found himself and was unburdened by the fear and anxiety of going broke. He could choose to work hard or go on vacation from a completely different orientation, one where his well-being was not outsourced to external events.

GOING DEEPER

When we begin questioning our thoughts and assumptions, it's important for us to stay with the process, even when initial answers are revealed. The reason for this continuation is that the subtext, the real reason why we do what we do, is often behind the initial answer. By asking, "What is it trying to make sure happens or doesn't happen? If that happens then what? And then what?" we are able to get to the underlying fear and ultimate intention of why we do what we do and why we think what we think.

SARAH

The desire for others to see us in a certain way is human nature. My friend Sarah wanted people to see her as someone who is always punctual. If she was ever late, she was worried that people would think she was inconsiderate, or that she didn't value their time. Underneath this was Sarah's fear of people not liking her. Even though she was consistently one of the first to arrive at the office every day, the minute she realized she would be late, for whatever reason, anxiety would immediately consume her. This angst would manifest itself physically as her body would begin to tighten. Her breath would shorten. With all this resistance activated, Sarah would judge herself and all the other drivers on the road, even if she was just a *little* late.

During one of our meetings, we drilled down on the fear and ended up with, "Then what if you end up alone because you got fired because people didn't like you for being late?" Sarah thought about this for a minute before finally answering, "I guess I'd be OK." Oftentimes, the "I'd be OK" answer can be overlooked, but there's value in allowing this recognition to sink in. I asked her to slow things down, bring up the anxiety of being late that was so familiar and simultaneously repeat out loud a few times, "I'd be OK." This has the potential to let the parts of our self that don't know they'd be OK to begin to really hear it. This can also provide the "space" we have been talking about for her to gain a little altitude from her contracted fear and realize there was a different way.

Sarah realized being late was not the end of the world, despite what her subconscious mind believed. It doesn't mean she wouldn't take responsibility and apologize for being late, and it doesn't mean she would stop her desire for punctuality. It simply meant Sarah could continue being on time as an expression of her values and how she wanted to show up instead of as a strategy to avoid experiencing the disapproval of others.

I have found that avoiding judgment from others is one of those unquestioned motivators that fuels us in life. Coincidentally, not long after our session, Sarah found herself running late to one of our mentoring sessions. This would mark the first time she was ever late. Life has an amusing way of testing us and repeating lessons we need to learn until we, in fact, learn them. I received a text from her that read, "Running 10 late, I'm sorry." When she arrived, she was calm and proceeded to tell me how she had caught herself panicking. She started to drive faster when the stress of being late washed over her. A thought of "this is the worst possible thing that could ever happen" began to overtake her. She caught herself in this old pattern and interrupted the chatter of her mind with a deep breath. Of course, she didn't like the fact she was running late, but she also knew she couldn't use me as an excuse to panic. She reminded herself of our session together and knew that I would be OK with her slight tardiness. This eventually made space for a great insight to come up. She realized the most honoring thing she could do for me and my time was to use the remaining minutes in traffic to calm herself down and arrive to our meeting fully centered and present.

I would rather have someone arrive ten minutes late to a meeting in a calm and present state than have them arrive on time but wrought with internal turmoil. I was grateful for her insight, because no matter the circumstances, we have a choice as to how we show up. Inner peace or chaos, it's always up to us. By using me as a test case, Sarah was able to shift away from her reactionary habit. I'm certain she's still one of the first to arrive at the office in the morning, though arriving on time is not always up to her. What is up to her is how she chooses to arrive, stressed or ready to crush it.

FACE THE SHIT

Shifting out of resistance brings us back to emotional fundamentals. In order for us to break free, we must be willing to experience whatever it is we are running away from. Our lives can be consumed by trying to avoid feelings like failure, rejection, or inadequacy, but this is a never-ending task. Remember the stick figure going after the carrot and being chased by the bag of shit?

If we truly want freedom, we must be willing to stop running, turn around, and let the stinky bag of shit catch up to us. The process of fully experiencing disappointment or regret is not necessarily comfortable, but if we can overcome our avoidance of what's uncomfortable, ultimately it will be freeing. We've all had difficult events and experienced disappointment or failure at some point in life, yet, as intense as these experiences were, they came and went and we're still here. Whatever is in our bag of shit, allowing ourselves to fully meet the one thing we're most invested in running away from liberates us from its intimidation. In my case, it was the feeling of inadequacy or unworthiness.

By being willing to explore our worst-case scenarios, we realize they are never as bad as we once imagined. We are like kids afraid of the monster or dragon lurking in our bedroom closet. The minute we find the courage to walk over and open the door, we see how those monsters are demystified. For some, this courage is readily available. For others, we need to work up to it before opening the door. Once we are able to be with our dragons, though, a lot of energy that was previously engaged in making sure the door remained closed is freed up.

With that being said, it's not always easy to face our dragons, as they're scary. We may first begin by avoiding the closet at all costs, going so far as to sleep in mom and dad's room. We may eventually muster the courage to sleep in our rooms again but block the closet door or maybe leave the lights on to help us fall asleep. We may feel safer by fantasizing our escape route if the monster does come out and "get us." We may even begin to imagine sounds coming from the closet, like the dragon is preparing to pounce the minute we close our eyes. Even when we have convinced ourselves the dragons aren't real, our mind and body remain on high alert. This may seem childish, but that's exactly how most of us approach our fears and the undesired possibilities in our lives; just look at all our anxiety, stress, and worry.

We don't have to spend our whole lives imprisoned by coping mechanisms and strategies to outrun scary dragons, though. When that kid is ready or has simply had enough of the running, he goes into the closet, even though he's afraid, and sleeps inside of it with the lights off. He wakes up the next morning and, after getting over the fact that he's still alive, smiles wide as he looks at the inside of the den from a whole new perspective. He feels empowered and capable of facing anything.

Most therapeutic approaches are oriented toward supporting people in becoming increasingly proficient at figuring out ways of escaping or fighting their dragons. However, there are core fixations at the heart of our humanity, like the feeling of not being enough, that no measure of affirmations, positive psychology, reframing, or other forms of therapy can unravel. This is because all these strategies are still operating from the premise that there's something that shouldn't be. What's required is a complete recognition of the futility of our efforts, a surrender so deep that all that is left is to bare our chest and let the dragon do its bidding.

Only at the moment in which we are willing to surrender all our strategies, face the monster, and let it devour us, again and again, does the dragon stop being scary. It was only frightening in the first place because we were so invested in avoiding it. Confronting our emotions isn't always comfortable, but it has the capacity to transform our lives. The only place we can confront them is where they manifest: in the body."

○

CHAPTER 9

PHYSICAL FREEDOM

The physical body is often referred to as a denser form of our being when compared to the subtle mental, emotional, and spiritual aspects of our experiences. Asceticism is seen in various forms in most major religions, and some traditions go as far as denouncing the body in an attempt to find liberation from the physical plane. While there is value in recognizing the wholeness of who we are is not limited to the physical body, it is important to acknowledge that our physicality is a direct expression of our essence. It provides a direct access point into the actual experience of the present moment and is therefore a great resource for breaking free from the egoic trance.

TUNING INTO THE BODY

The body holds an incredible amount of wisdom. If we pay attention, we can use it as a gateway to a more direct experience of reality than the one interpreted by thoughts and emotions. The mind works in time, but the body is always here. When our mind is heavily invested in avoiding a certain outcome, it often imagines negative future possibilities, and even though these dreadful things aren't actually happening, our body doesn't know. It thinks it's life or death and goes into high alert, as if our survival were at stake. When fear sets in, for example, the sympathetic nervous system gets activated to prepare us for "fight or flight."

Imagine you are going about your day and you suddenly receive an alarming text message that rattles you. You know the kind of text message I am referring to? It's the kind that pulls the rug right out from under your feet. When this happens, your mind will likely start spinning into fantasy thinking, and your body will respond in kind. Tightness in the chest. Shallow breathing. It's panic setting in, and your body has a whole protocol in place for these red flag moments.

The mechanisms that get triggered include the release of adrenaline and cortisol hormones, which can cause shortness of breath, chest pains, or even skin reactions. Your pupils may also dilate to allow in more light to spot a potential predator, the digestive system may slow down to conserve energy, and blood flow to the limbs may be rerouted to more important organs like the heart, which is no doubt jumping. It's survival time for the body, so it does whatever it has to do to persevere. There may be text messages that deserve that kind of response, but most of them don't.

Default reactions like these have their purpose, but we don't need to stop our digestion or dilate our pupils to respond to most of what life presents us with today. We can retrain how our body reacts to different circumstances, though, much in the same way we can relearn how to be with strong emotions. As with emotions, the challenge is that we've learned to cope with unwanted physical experiences by suppressing or ignoring them as much as possible, which only makes matters worse. Many of our physical conditions stem from this fundamentally unnatural approach. There is increasing scientific research that links chronic illness to this constriction of the energetic body. Dr. James W. Pennebaker, a social psychologist at the University of Texas at Austin, demonstrated this with his colleagues in 1997. He concluded, "Individuals who repress their emotions also suppress their body's immunity, making them more vulnerable to a variety of illnesses, ranging from common colds to cancer."

Why do we do that to our bodies? It's worth noting there's a difference between suppression and repression. Both involve denying impulses, but when we suppress, we are aware of what's going on and consciously reject the impulse. I'm angry but I'm not going to let myself get angry. With repression, we might not even be aware of what's going on. I'm angry, but I judge anger as unacceptable, so I unconsciously bypass it and, as it was in my case, go into victimhood. When we make a habit out of pushing down what we are feeling, we internalize an inefficient coping mechanism and turn suppression into repression. Our dysfunction is now unconscious and automatic. But that's OK, because we can unlearn all of this; we just need to pay close attention to the signals.

Our body is always communicating, so we might as well listen to what it is trying to tell us. In simplest terms, the body is a sensing mechanism through which we process environmental inputs and express them as outputs. It can be much like a microphone, taking in everything from the environment it is in. If we can nurture this connection, we realize it provides raw data about what's happening here and now, before it's interpreted by our eager commentator with its opinions and prejudices.

We have become so disconnected from the natural dialogue of our bodies, though, that we have begun to depend on technology as a proxy for our attention. The rise of wearable devices that monitor our steps, heart rate, sleep patterns, etc. has only just begun. Our watches and wristbands tell us how we feel, like contemporary versions of the mood ring. As an investor in some of these tech tools, I think they are amazing. But if we solely rely on them, we stand to further lose our organic connection to the body. We can use technology to complement our attentiveness but not to replace it. Our bodies have a lot to say, but if we stop listening, the subtle cues can eventually turn into physical ailments. What may have begun as a whisper will eventually scream.

MAKE CONTACT

Whenever my children experience a strong emotion, I invite them to pinpoint where they feel it in their body. Initially, my daughters had more direct access to what they were feeling and where they were feeling it than my son. Oftentimes, males tend to be more thinking and females more feeling.

Mothers run on feeling and emotion, and fathers, well, we "think" everything has a logical explanation. I've learned, despite my male stubbornness, to be a humble student of the females in my life.

As a child, and well into my young adult years, I was always in my head. The first time someone asked me where the emotion was in my body, I didn't know how to respond. It was like trying to flex a muscle I had never flexed before. To be brutally honest, I didn't even know the muscle existed. When we explore what something feels like physically, it is normal for the mind to become active and "think" about or label what is happening. The overexercised muscle compensates for the weaker muscle. The mind is used to running the show.

Developing the ability to bring your physical sensations into the foreground is vital to freeing ourselves from unconscious patterns. The more we're in touch with them, the more conscious we become. I invite my kids to identify specific qualities in what they are feeling. I ask questions like: "What does anger or loneliness feel like in your body? Where exactly are you feeling it?" Sometimes we feel these sensations in our heart, gut, or head. Sometimes it feels like the sensations have taken over the body completely.

Over time, we develop the ability to go even deeper by exploring the feeling's size, texture, and color. I ask the kids if the physical sensation has anything it wants to share. Doing this work with children is revelatory, not only for them, but for me as well. Sometimes, I have observed them having full-on conversations with their sensations. When asked what the feeling was trying to say about loneliness in her chest, my daughter gave it a voice: "I don't want to be alone. I want to make friends." To which she replied, "I'm trying, but I want to find some really, really good friends."

Adults have learned to dismiss opportunities like these. We stay in our mind and become detached to what the body is trying to tell us. It would make us feel far too vulnerable to admit that we feel lonely sometimes. It is possible, however, to unwind these tendencies and meet our vulnerabilities, desires, and concerns with greater openness.

LOOKING FOR LOVE

What the feeling of loneliness is basically saying, after all, is, "I want to be loved." Most of us relate to this kind of sensation by ignoring it or looking for someone or something to make us feel whole. Emotions like this stem from parts of us that were likely hurt when we were younger. We may have bought into the terrible misunderstanding that we are unlovable and desperately look for others to prove the belief wrong. These emotional fractures have a way of sticking with us as we grow up, particularly when we continue reinforcing the "unlovability" by disregarding the sensations.

Whenever we push away feelings or try to bury them with avoidance or escapism, they congeal into nodes or points within the physical body. When left unattended, they become knots; the more we resist, the tighter they get. In order for these atrophied points to loosen and return to their natural flow, we must release our antagonistic relationship with them and knead them with the acceptance they've been looking for. Like a river that has accumulated debris, our body is always looking for a way to keep flowing; it has an aliveness to it. When the passages are blocked, it must find another outlet or eventually lose its vitality. Our bodies know what to do; we just need to come into harmony with them and allow energy to circulate more naturally.

This is not something reserved for yogis or even advanced students of meditation. It's a simple practice that anyone willing can do at any time. Whenever we find our thoughts spinning, we can just take a breath and ask ourselves, "What is my experience of right now? Where is it happening in the body?" If the answer is, "I don't know," then the invitation is to experience what the "I don't know" sensation feels like, even if it's just in the head. The important thing is to not judge the answers but to remain open. The mind doesn't like to be bypassed, so it may jump from one thought to another. This is normal. If this happens for you, then simply be aware of the darting and ask yourself, "What does all this darting around feel like?" The invitation is to continuously come back to "now" through the body. This immediately takes you from the mental whirlpool of fantasyland and into a more grounded, real, and present experience.

Awareness of what the body is experiencing is the first step in disentangling it from the egoic grip. Awareness can be a double-edged sword, though. When we initially become attentive to our body, we're consciously slowing down and suspending our usual coping mechanisms. That can be very uncomfortable, because we have trained ourselves not to feel or be aware of what we have determined to be undesirable.

It's therefore important to remain conscious and not go into judgment of the sensation because that puts us back into resistance. The remedy is to remain very curious.

THE DEEP DISCOMFORT

I never truly learned how to be with strong sensations. There's a difference between experiencing something in our bodies and telling ourselves a story about it. Shame is one of those strong sensations that I was programmed to avoid at all costs. Instead of feeling the shame directly, I would go into self-judgment or jump straight into justification. Shame was just the byproduct of something deeper, though the underlying wound was inadequacy.

Remember repression? I was so sophisticated at denying inadequacy that I even hid it from myself. I used to say, "Inadequate? Me? Absolutely not! I am amazing. I have well-deserved and healthy self-esteem." The thing I hadn't faced, however, was how afraid I was of tapping into my own sense of unworthiness. Because of this, I was completely invested in proving how extraordinary I was.

It took me a while to find the willingness to face this core wound. I had done just fine navigating my way around it, so why should I go in and start poking around? Thankfully, I eventually came to see all the ways it was impacting my life. It had become like the stone in my shoe and something I learned to live with. Sure, I could leave it in there, but the minute I knew it was there, I could feel it with every step.

If I was going to connect with shame, I needed to recall situations which reminded me of the sensation. There were certain memories which would make me blush by just thinking of them; they were those moments where all I wanted to do was hide. It really didn't matter which one I picked; like branches of a tree, all eventually led back to the trunk of inadequacy.

I grew up very familiar with shame. I used to wet my bed way past what seemed "normal" for boys my age and was convinced I was the only eleven-year-old who still had these sorts of "accidents." My mom took me to the family doctor so they could try and figure out what was happening; as far as I could tell, there was something definitely wrong with me. My parents tried all sorts of strategies from punishment to reward to "fix" the problem. In the end, however, none of these strategies helped. Waking up to a wet bed was terrifying and sleeping with a plastic cover under my sheets was embarrassing, especially when friends would come over to play. I was afraid to go on overnight trips or join friends when one of them had a slumber party, so I would always make up excuses for missing them.

I was petrified when I found out I was being sent to boarding school. To aggravate my concerns, I had to share a bunk bed with a kid who was fourteen years old and very scary. At that age, a couple years make a big difference. He bullied me about little things, so the idea of wetting my bed and him finding out was terrifying. Waking up in the middle of the night and frantically trying to change the sheets so he wouldn't notice produced a tremendous amount of angst.

I wasn't capable of meeting shame directly at that time, so anxiety became my default state, and suppression turned into repression. This inner turmoil created a new set of instructions in my system: I must hide my defectiveness because if people find out, I'm in big trouble. Repression makes our programming run automatically; it operates even when the situation doesn't merit that kind of response—oh and it doesn't have an expiration date. As an adult, I was still being run by this mandate and continuously trying to seem perfect. I had done a lot of therapy and psychological work to heal this, but that was always geared toward making myself feel better by normalizing the situation and getting rid of the feeling. If I wanted freedom, I had to be willing to face the thing I was trying to avoid all along, feeling defective.

I thought about one of those uncomfortable memories and let the sensations come to the surface. At first, I noticed the stories I was accustomed to hearing, both the sad ones and the ones that told me I was just a little boy and how there was a lot going on in my household at the time. Nevertheless, I found a way to stay with the raw sensation. I was in memory, but the experience and sensations were happening in my grown-up body, like the juicy lemon example. It felt intense, but I knew I had to surrender all attempts at controlling this and let it have its way with me. My face flushed as I recalled the feelings and saw images of my childhood friends inquiring about the way my bed smelled. I was right there with my eleven-year-old self and witnessed the thought of "something is wrong with me" and the desire to lie to my friends about how my dog had just peed in the carpet come up. I didn't go there and let the discomfort reach its peak. I was in the experience of my younger self but was connected with the resourcefulness of my adult self simultaneously. I was in the closet with the dragon and the lights were off.

After the storm passed, my eleven-year-old kind of looked around and realized he had faced the un-faceable and was still standing. It sounds silly, but it was cathartic; I had felt the sense of inadequacy fully, and yet instead of feeling crushed, I felt liberated. Like a refrigerator that suddenly stops humming, I didn't realize how much effort was invested and wasted in avoiding the sense of "I'm not good enough" until it wasn't there anymore. It's not that the sense of inadequacy would never arise again, but rather that I now knew I could face it. The resulting effect was a drastic change in my behavior, inside and out.

WELCOMING JEALOUSY

One of the ways in which inadequacy made itself apparent was through jealousy. I really judged myself for this, because it did not fit my idea of a confident and conscious man. While feeling unworthy was repressed and kept unconscious, jealousy was something I was very aware of and consciously submerged. I managed to avoid the sensation by investing a lot of my energy into the appearance of being an amazing man in the eyes of others, particularly my partner. As long as I was always "the best" in her eyes, I was able to feel safe.

I would constantly scan my environment for threats and manage how I was seen by others. I believed the more desirable people perceived me to be, the less chance there was for me to experience betrayal. I remember even feeling a sense of relief when I discovered a girlfriend's platonic celebrity crush was, in fact, gay. The idea of not being the most "everything" to my partner meant I could be, at some point, replaced. My sense of identity was attached to how needed and desired I was.

I did a lot of therapeutic work around this issue and recognized that it originated from how I perceived the dynamic of my parents' relationship growing up. Because my siblings and I were still very young, our parents decided it was best if they kept the family unit intact as opposed to getting a divorce. What we didn't know was that Mom and Dad were no longer romantic and had their own arrangement in which they could lead separate and ongoing romantic lives outside of the marriage. To me, this was extremely confusing. It created a lot of misunderstandings, especially where loyalty and trust were concerned.

It made perfect sense why I experienced a lack of trust in my own intimate relationships. I was constantly on the lookout for a shoe to drop, because I was under the impression that my parents were disloyal to each other. Years into my psychological and spiritual development, and despite focusing on healing this part of me, jealousy still felt crippling. At one point, I realized all the work I had done was focused on getting rid of jealousy. I had developed sophisticated strategies for managing or denying the existence of it, but I had never really faced this particular dragon.

While the exploration of inadequacy was something I went into willingly, this wasn't a door I ever wanted to open. Toward the end of a ten-day silent meditation retreat and through the sheer exhaustion caused by all my resistance around the subject, I finally gave in. It wasn't a new strategy that finally made room for this change but rather a tiredness from running. One of the benefits of retreats is that they wear your ego down; it's harder to avoid things because there are fewer distractions. It felt like I had been running from a bully for a long time, and finally I just made a decision to stop running. I stopped running not because I wasn't afraid of the bully but because I was exhausted from all the running. My defenses were down and all I could do was brace for it. It came in waves of contraction, nausea, stomach pain, and a pressed heart. Interestingly enough, those were very familiar sensations. They were the exact same feelings I experienced every time I resisted jealousy. What's even crazier is that they were also the exact feelings jealousy itself was trying to prevent from arising by protecting me from a future where my partner could cheat on me. Talk about locking myself up in a circular reference of torment. Another case of suffer *now* so you don't suffer *then*.

Once jealousy was allowed to exist without conditions, something inside shifted. In the same way it happened with inadequacy, as intimidating as this bully was, when jealousy caught up to me, it didn't kill me. I was familiar with the strong sensations of jealousy in the pit of my stomach, but without making them "wrong" by immediately defaulting to one of my many coping mechanisms, they were quite tolerable. The more I loosened my grip, the more my stomach and gut relaxed. The more I welcomed it, the more life energy got freed up.

It turns out that jealousy, as undesirable as it was, is also just an energy at its essence. It was almost like I had trapped a small animal and confined it to a cage. That containment was the reason why my jealousy was so uncomfortable. I was managing the feeling and preventing it from having space to be. When I opened up the lock, this little monster was finally able to have its liberty, so it stopped rattling the cage.

Jealousy has reared its head a few times since that experience. And as with any massive shift, there were some knee-jerk reactions to avert it and say to myself, "Not again." But once you have slept in the closet with the dragon, things are never the same. I knew this was an old pattern of resistance, and I could now recognize it as completely unnecessary.

I now have an open-door policy where jealousy is concerned. Like an old acquaintance who knows where I live, it may or may not show up again in my life, but this openness seems to keep it from visiting. Resistance is like a magnet that brings forward whatever is not fully allowed within us.

GOING DEEPER

Once I realized it was possible to stop running away from things, I began to identify other experiences I had never allowed myself to fully feel. So, I began to experiment. The next time I was hungry, I asked myself, "What does it really feel like to be hungry?" I was so trained to get food whenever

I felt hungry, it became nothing more than a signal or alert saying, "It's time to eat."

I noticed I would get moody or come down with a slight headache whenever I didn't get food quickly enough. Thanks to the youthful wisdom of my kids, they informed me this is known as being "hangry." Whatever name you want to give it, the reaction does makes sense, because lack of food requires immediate action. It may still be the case for many people on this planet, but that's not my current reality.

It was astounding to realize I had lived so long without ever fully connecting to something so basic. I now understand how being hungry is like being jealous. They are both energies manifesting themselves in the body which I had learned to avoid. Hunger was actually easier to meet, because I hadn't attached my identity to it. However, even though the ways of avoiding the two sensations are different, the premise is essentially the same.

As with jealousy, when I fully experienced the feeling of being hungry, I realized there was a raw aliveness to the energy. The more I allowed myself to feel the feeling itself, the more my body learned how to relax around it. What I had previously labeled as hunger had actually been the byproduct of thoughts like, "I have to do something about this," with the accompanying headache, contraction, or anxiety as I counted the minutes until the next meal. This was different. Since that day, I relate to hunger as a visiting energy that carries information but no longer has a negative connotation. I used to have to eat throughout the day; now

I fast most days for about sixteen hours and hunger is more of a gentle nudge.

Another body sensation I found myself exploring was that of fatigue. I'm sure we can all relate to the sensation of feeling tired (Parenting 101). Whenever I experienced tiredness, I would immediately complain. I was a victim of my fatigue! I found myself approaching it as something that needed fixing. "Why am I tired? It's the middle of the day. I thought I got enough sleep last night. I should get some coffee or find some other way to be more awake." Again, I was resisting what was happening. Like hunger, being tired was an experience I felt I needed to avoid. As quickly as possible, I needed to shift out of the sensation, either by ignoring it or consuming some kind of caffeinated energy drink.

When I became willing to experience tiredness directly, the sensation was actually quite pleasant. Being tired became something I now felt in the front of my face, the droopiness of my eyes, and the relaxation of my shoulders. When I allowed myself to feel tired, I would actually enjoy it and sometimes just sit or lie down. It didn't matter if I was someplace where it didn't feel completely appropriate to do so. I would just honor what being tired felt like, even if it was for only a few seconds. I wasn't taking a "power nap" or anything like that. I was simply saying "yes" rather than "no" to what was happening in my now moment.

I finally learned how to become intimate with a feeling I had had all my life but never really allowed myself to experience in its fullness. Being tired became one more experience to be with, rather than a nuisance to get over. I was meeting it as a manifestation of my body's wisdom, rather than something I needed to change or get rid of. The more we can accept what we are experiencing, by questioning the need to fix it, the more at peace we can be.

This dynamic also occurred with what I consider to be a positive and natural sensation, the sex drive. *Hello.* As with hunger or tiredness, I used to immediately follow the feeling of being "turned on" with the thought, "I need to do something about this." When I allowed myself to experience being attracted to a woman without feeling compelled to do anything about it, I began to discover how attraction was a feeling in its own right. It was another sensation that could be granted permission to be fully here and not something to be dealt with.

For most of my life, I had related to the energies in my body as nothing more than prompts for me to do something about, rather than as experiences to be felt and honored. This new approach was incredibly liberating. Whenever I stopped investing myself in the need to act in response to these "prompts," a tremendous amount of energy was freed up; it was like finally swimming downstream. Our body can be incredibly useful in providing insights and will always give us direct feedback of whatever is happening, but it's one thing to listen to the body and its messages and another to convert everything into some kind of "to-do."

The takeaway here is our acknowledgment of the body's incredible wisdom and the way our thoughts and misconceptions have a way of disrupting the organic flow. When I'm not feeling well, a question I like to ask is, "What am

I doing or believing that might be getting in the way of my body reharmonizing itself?" More often than not, it is usually some thought form that is resisting what happened or trying to control what could happen. My body may feel tired when I push it too hard. My mind, however, thinks I should be operating as usual, so my body doesn't get the downtime needed for replenishment. Without my notions of what should and shouldn't be, my body instinctively knows what to do. The key is to listen.

(RE)HARMONIZING THE ENERGY FLOW

Physical freedom enables the rebalancing of the body and its natural tendency toward coherence. It does this by circulating energy that has been trapped or contained and allowing it to flow effortlessly. The energy in our bodies has a natural path, like water in a stream. When we're not trying to control it, its movement becomes open and unrestricted.

I know when I'm getting a cold, because I feel that tingling in the back of the throat, which often signals a sore throat is coming. My immediate reaction used to be, "Oh, no, I'm about to get sick. I've got to do something about this. There are so many reasons why it would be bad for me to get a cold right now. Is it because my son was sneezing when he got back from school?" The mind will always look for a logical explanation, especially the male reptilian brain, to whatever is happening or about to happen. It wants to fix things.

I was saying *no* to what I was actually experiencing. As I became aware of this, I decided to look at it from a different perspective. I got really curious with the tingling feeling at the back of my throat. What is it like to feel the tingling directly, before imposing a meaning on the sensation or drawing some final conclusion? I became interested in what was happening, what that experience was like, instead of immediately jumping in to "address" what I was feeling. I realized the tingling was the way my body was doing its part. It meant that blood vessels were dilating to let more white blood cells flow into the infected tissues. Instead of complaining about the soreness, I saw it as a reminder that my body knows how to take care of itself.

Homeostasis is defined as the ability of an organism to maintain a state of internal balance and physical well-being in spite of changes or external factors. By trying to manage and resist the symptoms, I was essentially blocking the inherent way in which my system orients itself back to health. Meeting the "symptoms" with openness keeps me from instinctively jumping in and intervening in this natural process. I may still "have a cold," but many times the cold never really shows up. If it does, and additional symptoms appear, I allow my body to experience the "symptoms" or physical manifestations as openly as I can. That experience can include crankiness, body aches, and a number of other unpleasant feelings, but even those can be allowed to exist.

This doesn't mean we give up our capacity to take appropriate action whenever necessary. I may still choose to take medication or go to a doctor when appropriate, but I'm making more space for my body to do what it inherently needs to do, which is balance itself. By bringing greater awareness to our impulses, we can unlearn the habit of layering resistance on top of what is already happening. A cold, without the antagonism for the cold, is a lot less unpleasant.

The human body is one of the wonders of nature. It can heal and repair itself, if allowed the space and time in order to do so. We can use the mind to help us support the body, but we have been wired to use the body to support the mind's agenda. By unburdening our body from the tyranny of the mind, we restore it to its natural faculties and make it possible for what can be called our spirit to be more fully embodied.

CHAPTER 10

SPIRITUAL FREEDOM

*My religion consists of a humble admiration of the illimitable
superior spirit who reveals himself in the slight details we are
able to perceive with our frail and feeble mind.*
—ALBERT EINSTEIN, Theoretical physicist

Approaching the intense turbulence and persistent grip
of human conditioning with a restorative attitude could
be called "psychological freedom." Most of what we've covered in the book up to now is in this domain and is aimed
at having a healthier sense of self. Therapy, counseling, and
other self-help modalities are phenomenal resources that
help attain the relative freedom that reduces stress, boosts
self-esteem, and helps overcome misunderstandings and
past wounding. The healthier our sense of self is, the more
pleasant our journey becomes, for ourselves and those
around us.

I have had a lot of experience with this kind of work, and even though I have found it truly valuable, it also has its limitations. People can spend decades in therapy and still have deep unconscious wounds and misunderstandings operating in their day-to-day lives. Our mind likes to feel useful, so it can use healing as a way to turn us into a never-ending self-improvement project. This approach, however, ultimately originates from the basic misunderstanding that we are somehow broken. Eventually, what's needed is to discover a larger perspective from which we can perceive our fundamental unbrokenness. When our perception is no longer fixated on our egoic identity, we can release our fascination with noticing what's wrong and the subsequent fascination with trying to fix it.

PEELING THE LAYERS

Spirituality can mean different things for different people. For me, it is the recognition of the deeper context within which our reality unfolds. Growing up, I was enthralled with the people in the congregation who committed themselves to a life of service and devotion to their version of a deeper context. I connected with Christ as the ultimate embodiment and image of love and compassion, but I had questions. I had a lot of questions.

I went to a Catholic elementary school and remember being confused by the well-intended but ultimately convoluted answers to the many doubts I had. My science teacher, who was also a priest, seemed to be having just as much trouble as I was understanding who came first, Adam and Eve or

SPIRITUAL FREEDOM • 171

the cavemen. At some point, blind faith wasn't satisfying enough for me; I felt there was something more to explore. I was intensely curious about life's grand questions, but it seemed wrong to doubt, because I was told questioning those teachings was a sinful act.

I soon became disenchanted with Catholicism and was skeptical of all religions and what they stood for. Like a teenager rebelling against his parents, I pushed the church away and began to judge any religious institution as an unnecessary intermediary to God. This is right about the time I began to shift my contemplative focus to those I considered to be enlightened masters. In this pursuit, however, I simply recreated the same thing I was running away from in Catholicism. The intermediary now became these new symbols of perfection, those I had come to put on a pedestal, as the standard for how I should be.

My journey was propelled by the desire to be happy. I felt guilty admitting this even to myself because, objectively speaking, I was aware of how blessed I was. Everything about my life was so good, at least on the outside. The inside, however, was unsettled. I was lost inside of myself not knowing who I was or who I was supposed to be. I never had to worry about not having enough to eat or a place to lay my head at night, but I felt subtly discontented with this "good" life. My feelings of disconnection seemed selfish, though. I mean, how ungrateful to have so much and still want even more, especially when others were having such a difficult time in life. Despite all my attempts at denial, the feeling that something was missing added an indisputable rattle and hum to my existence. Spirituality became my avenue for exploring this sense of dissatisfaction as I asked questions nobody seemed to have answers to.

BEYOND THE PERSONA

If we are to be spiritually free, we have to be willing to question some of the most elementary assumptions about life and who we have deemed ourselves to be. The egoic mind will try and hold on for dear life to the ideas it has about itself, so be prepared to experience a lot of resistance as you question these beliefs. It will use all sorts of arguments to keep the status quo from shifting. Ultimately, the ego will fight for its survival.

The ego is not the bad guy here. It's just the part of us that hasn't caught up to the fact that we are limitless. However, as long as the sense of separation with identities that need to be maintained and protected remains at the center of our experience, we are still hindered by its agenda. If I define myself though these masks, I will become invested in preserving them. Existential crises usually result when some of our dearest identities are challenged. It's like we have been dressing up in costumes but forgot that we are, in fact, dressed up.

When we start questioning our identities and taking them off, we think that the next persona is the "real me" because we have layers upon layers. The deeper our work, the more subtle and convincing the next mask is. True spiritual inquiry is the investigation into who or what is underneath all those masks.

Throughout my life, even before consciously embarking on a spiritual path, I experienced what I would now call moments of deep connection. These were instances when the masks came off, the veil of conditioned "reality" lifted and everything became lighter. The framework of me and you lost its solidity and the interconnectedness of all was vividly apparent. I didn't assign much meaning to these glimpses at the time, because I wasn't yet a "card-carrying spiritual seeker." Later on, with a more developed spiritual ego, I became invested in getting out from behind that veil for good and having my entire life be made up of these experiences. Of course, as tends to happen when we chase something, they stopped happening as often. Even though my mind highjacked the spontaneous nature of these early experiences, they remained valuable reference points throughout my life for the prospect of a different reality.

These moments of deep spiritual connection would often take place when I found myself in nature, reading a book, or being of service to others. The common denominator in these quiet moments was a sense of devotion and calm, where the "me," my sense of self, took a back seat to the present-moment experience.

Long after my disenchantment with institutionalized religion, I would often go to church, not to attend mass, but to sit and contemplate the quietness of an environment I felt a strong connection with. At the time, I didn't realize this was actually a form of meditation. Turns out I was great at meditating, until I actually *tried* to meditate.

THE GREAT DIVINE

For me, and I'm sure for many others, the sense that there might be something greater than ourselves has the ability to provide a tremendous amount of comfort. It eases the fear that arrives when we realize we are not in control of our lives. It becomes a Band-Aid applied to the fear of death that is so pervasive, especially in Western cultures. Many seekers are motivated to have spirituality become their guide, and they believe their behavior will have an effect on how they are judged, rewarded, or punished.

This attitude is not "wrong" in and of itself. Depending on circumstances, we may need positive or negative reinforcement to motivate us to conduct ourselves in certain ways. At some point, however, we evolve out of our need for an externalized directive and venture into a direct discovery of the mystery of existence.

True spirituality puts us in contact with something beyond the rational understanding of our minds. Growing up, some of us referred to this as a "higher power, God, or divinity." It is also referred to by many other names: love, the universe, consciousness, etc. I was always impressed by how Christianity speaks of God as omniscient and omnipresent. Although this is never debated or questioned in religious discussions, it often seems to exist alongside a sense or feeling of selectiveness or judgment: "This is divine, and that is not divine. This is an act of God, and that is not. This is God, and that is the devil."

As you can imagine, I found all of this extremely confusing. I mean, I understood omniscient and omnipresent to mean that there is nowhere and nothing that God is not. If there is nothing that God is not, then hunger, jealousy, the pounds we want to lose, and the person we judge the most are all God. When we approach life this way, the whole game of duality and opposites, the game of heaven and hell, begins to collapse.

> *Out beyond ideas of wrong-doing and right-doing,*
> *there is a field. I'll meet you there.*
> —RUMI, Persian mystic poet

That field Rumi speaks of is what I believe is meant by the phrase "heaven on earth." It certainly feels like a more natural way of being than hanging out in the subjective experience of what should or shouldn't be. When we are in that place of equanimity, life just feels good. The mind, however, will justify judgment because it thinks seeing "love in all" is somehow irresponsible. It thinks we will become complacent and that somehow the order will collapse, and everything will fall into chaos. Recognizing everything is "one with life," however, does not mean we lose our capacity to discern and make intelligent choices in the same way that a parent's infinite love for their children doesn't stifle their judgment.

CRUTCHES

It is probably impossible to avoid idealization on the spiritual journey, whether it be teachers, teachings, spiritual states, or enlightenment concepts. For me, the soul was one such concept. I would define the soul as consisting entirely of what is good or the "best in us," as something divine and beyond our ego. This is a valuable reference, but it can also be a trapdoor along the spiritual path. It can provide a refined and purified safe haven for the new identity to lodge itself in. "I am my soul," reinforces the experience of a separate self, even if it's a more spiritual one. Unchecked, it can still be used as a subtle way of separating ourselves from life and providing our egos with a place to set up shop.

The concept of "soul" is similar to the concept of God, if God is all that we believe to be good projected onto an idealized and external figure. Don't get me wrong, this idealization can be extremely valuable and even necessary along our journey. However, as a concept, it can also become constricting, and, if so, it needs to be examined. The idealized, externalized image of the soul or of God is only a reference point for our deepest essence. This is integrated through the recognition that there is absolutely no separation between our soul, this godliness, and our moment-to-moment "normal" life. All are animated by and inseparable from the same source.

What might be called "soul liberation" is actually a form of self-liberation. When we are ready to let go of all concepts and recognize the need for a different kind of faculty, an autonomy beyond all concepts comes online. The next stage on the path requires us to let go of all externalized references and rely on our curiosity as our only compass. Although this is not a linear process with a clear set of guidelines or steps to follow, there are ingredients that I have found to be valuable along the way. Meditation, self-inquiry, stillness, deep contemplation, and a good dose of courage, humility, and humor have been essential for me.

In matters of religion, most persons prefer chewing the menu to actually eating the food!
—ZEN SAYING

MEDITATION AND THOUGHT BUBBLES

Meditation is defined as a practice where an individual uses a technique—such as mindfulness or focusing on a particular object, thought, or activity—to train attention and awareness and achieve a mentally clear and emotionally calm and stable state. Yes, maybe on some level, but it's much more than that. This is like saying the whole purpose of praying is to get what you want. As I see it, meditation is more of a way to fully inhabit the moment. In its purest expression, it is the simple act of being…here…now.

Most spiritual traditions have some form of meditation as part of their daily rituals, not necessarily in the conventional sense of the seated lotus position, but in other forms like silence, mantras, focused prayer, dancing, chanting, and/or visualization. In a sense, meditation is a devotional practice, although not to any particular figure or ideal. It's a devotion to life as we encounter and live it in the present moment. For me, it's much more akin to my spontaneous childhood moments of quiet than to my mostly failed attempts at "sitting still and quieting the mind."

In our modern ways, we have turned meditation into a tool to counterbalance stress and calm our system. As useful as that can be, when we approach meditation as a technique for exerting our agenda, it can become another way to put demands on the moment. The gift of meditation is how it brings us closer to life as it is at any given moment, and thereby highlights how we push back against it. When we make meditation into a thing we do, to achieve a particular state and get someplace other than our here and now, we're caught in the loop of resistance.

It seems to me that we all inherently know how to meditate. It's only our ideas of what meditation should look like that get in the way. When I first started attending meditation retreats, I would hear the sound of the bell to begin a session and would immediately "get ready to meditate." I would sit up straight, fix my posture, take a deep breath, and get ready. I was metaphorically rolling up my sleeves and saying, "OK, let's do this." It's funny to me now, but I dreaded the process.

It is so much easier to look at meditation as "just being." What I mean by that is to essentially be with *what is*, without an agenda, judgment or manipulation of whatever *is*.

If meditation involves any sort of strategy, it would be a subtle commitment not to indulge the thinking mind and notice whenever we are caught in thought. Upon the realization, we just let the thought and the realization go. When you first realize you've been caught in a thought or story, it's quite natural to think you shouldn't be thinking. As you might have guessed, this is itself just another thought.

Some people use mantras or breathing techniques to shift out of their habitual thinking paradigm, but I used soap bubbles. Sounds silly, but for me, the image of soap bubbles worked best. You see, I would view thoughts as shiny bubbles which floated up into my awareness. Whenever I noticed one of these thought bubbles, I imagined popping them. Sometimes, this process happened after only a few seconds. Other times, it happened after much time lost in the trance of thinking. The funny thing about this exercise is how some bubbles arrived with convincing authority. They would justify their existence even after I became aware of them. I would hear things like, "No, I can't pop this one, I can't afford to forget this." I have heard many arguments along the way, but I never regretted popping a thought bubble.

I became an active and diligent "thought-bubble popper." It gave the mind something to do, which at the beginning helped me stick with meditation. It was a useful tool for me to clear the cloudy skies before I could fully embrace the totality of it, clouds and all.

Eventually, these thought bubbles stopped rising up and would collapse as soon as they began to form. I began to notice how my thoughts only existed and became validated when I engaged them. When I stopped participating, the thought bubbles simply lost their buoyancy. From this point, the process became quieter and less active. My thought bubbles would arrive and pass away without the need for any of my popping. They were merely thoughts and not facts, so they would ultimately dissipate from my awareness.

What became critical for me was to not view a meditation without bubbles as successful or viewing one that looked like a bubble-bath party as unsuccessful. For me, meditation was a way of prioritizing the state of just being and developing my capacity to be with what was, not a measure of how good or effective that capacity became.

Meditation shifted from a technique meant to help me experience something in particular into a deep reverence for life and the moment. I now hold it as a form of settling into a natural state, where there is a deep intimacy with…well, pretty much everything. This reverence for life as it shows up in this and every moment, is the ultimate arms-wide-open embrace, encompassing everything and excluding nothing. I know this can seem quite esoteric to grasp onto, but it's not too dissimilar from how we all related to the world as children, with openness and curiosity. A prayerful meditation practice reminds us what it's like to embrace all of it…always, and in all ways.

SELF-INQUIRY

Spiritual inquiry is the process of investigating our beliefs through our direct experience and challenging some of the core unquestioned assumptions we have been living out of. If knowledge is the process of actively looking for answers, inquiry involves a more contemplative approach, one which allows the kind of questions that take us to the edge of spiritual understanding to arise.

Because it is uncomfortable to sit with deep existential dilemmas, it is important to become aware of the mind's urge to fill the void with the *right* answer. Sitting with the evoking stillness is much more valuable than the resolution we try to come to. Questions like, "What is life? What is actually true in my direct experience? What is time? What or who is God? Who am I?" are like little cracks, chipping away at the dam of what is known, and they are at the heart of genuine spiritual inquiry and exploration. I know this is getting heavy, but the actual purpose of these questions is to take us beyond what we can comprehend intellectually and lead us on an adventure of personal discovery.

Not that long ago, if you were curious about spirituality, you would have to travel long distances, decipher hidden texts, or subscribe to particular rituals and/or traditions. You would have to work hard to earn your way to the nuggets of revelation and insight. Thankfully, in today's society, these teachings are merely a click away. We are bombarded with concepts and insights that our modern mind can easily digest. Take this book, for example. Like any other book on the subject, there isn't anything here that one would consider groundbreaking. Some people find the teachings of *The Power of Now* by Eckhart Tolle difficult to digest, while others might read a dense text like *The Bhagavad Gita* and devour it. That's the beauty of the commonality of what's being said—they are different ways of saying the same thing. This book is a simple attempt at pointing to *what is* from a different perspective...my perspective.

What we often fail to realize is that teachings aren't meant to give us the answer to the spiritual questions. They are more like road signs along our way which are meant to stump or prompt our own self-reflection. I was lucky enough to have a vast array of teachers who didn't claim any sort of "godlike" specialness. They would give me back my own authority every time I gave it to them by putting them on a pedestal. They referred to themselves as merely the breadcrumbs along my spiritual path. They never viewed themselves as a gateway to anyone else's freedom. All the great mystics and teachers who have walked before us have carved their own paths. Through their journeys, they simply nudge us, guide us, and invite us to do the same.

CHAPTER 11

○

WAKING UP

In order to arrive at what you are not,
you must go through the way in which you are not.
And what you do not know is the only thing you know.
—T. S. ELIOT, Nobel Prize in Literature (1948)

My spiritual drive was fueled by the desire for more freedom. I know, there's that word again, "more." I was convinced this was a journey where my separate, independent identity would become a spiritually evolved, perfect, and ideal version of itself. But, as fate would have it, this was just another example of the "Pac-Man" programming doing what it has been trained to do, accumulate. Its objective was now more wisdom, more certainty, more answers, more love, more peace. More, more, more. There was no mistake that I was a committed seeker, because all my type A energy was now channeled toward raising my level of consciousness. I wanted an advanced or high-enough state where I would be like one of those awakened masters I so looked up to and idolized. Then, and only then, would I conquer this thing called life, perpetually inhabiting an untouched state of continuous bliss.

I had heard there were levels assigned to various states, and that different spiritual systems have even named these stages to indicate the degree of realization. David R. Hawkins, MD, PhD, author of *Power vs. Force*, even developed a Map of Consciousness which defined a range of values that correspond to a set of levels with a logarithmic scale from one to 1,000. For example, Christ and Buddha were at 1,000, Mahatma Gandhi was at 760, and Picasso was at 365. Since I am an overachiever, it was great fuel for my ego, because the mind loves measuring things, and mine had found a new metric for success. I found myself focusing all my energy on achieving and maintaining as heightened a state of awareness as humanly possible.

While some of it was beautiful, it was also high maintenance. I was approaching enlightenment the same way I had approached everything else in life, full throttle. I would know when I got there because I would be in a perfect and permanent state of mind-blowing oneness and elation. My concept of enlightenment was conditioning life to just continual peace and bliss; it was still pretending to know what life should be like. Much in the same way psychologically oriented modalities try and perfect the self, spiritual seekers often want to become enlightened enough to bypass the self. But that's just more of the same egoic drive trying to avoid dealing with what it deems unpleasant in our all-too-human humanity.

However self-centered it may have been, this attitude was actually what drove me to spend a lot of time in silence and deep contemplation. I began to submerse myself in reading books on self-realization and explore different spiritual lineages and teachings. Walking this part of the path had many gifts. One gift in particular was the altitude or "higher perspective" through which I could begin to have distance from my day-to-day struggles. The goal was now to get to as high an altitude as possible so my day-to-day life would no longer hurt or feel burdensome. The problem is that this became just another way of coping. In essence, it was the spiritual equivalent of drinking or using TV to avoid hardship.

I remember one night lying in bed feeling extremely enlightened and suddenly recognizing, in horror I might add, that I was not as free as I thought. My spiritual journey had been turned into an egoic crusade. The insights and realizations were the new precious bank account that defined my value and self-worth. It was still all about the ego's agenda and its attempts at controlling life. If I wanted to discover an unconditional freedom, I had to be willing to unravel the entire framework of the egoic self.

THE DREAM

When we're dreaming at night, there is usually a protagonist whom we base our dream reality around. Within this dream, the protagonist's fears and desires seem of utmost importance, but it's all made up; it's in our heads. We take ourselves to be this character with its identity and agendas, but we're so much more than that; we're the one who's dreaming it all.

Self-realization is often talked about as waking up from the egoic dream. It's the recognition that the persona we have based our whole reality around is analogous to the protagonist in our sleeping dream. We think this is who we are, but our sense of individualized identity is also just a character. No matter how much things have changed for this character, there has always been a constant, a dreamer if you will, witnessing it all.

If the "me" we believe ourselves to be is just part of the changing phenomena within that dream, then who or what is the one who is dreaming? When I first looked for that "dreamer," I came up with a sense of "I" as an answer. I figured somewhere inside of me there was an "I" that had always been aware of all the things that had ever happened in my life. Then I realized there even had to be something aware of that sense of I to begin with, like an always-present consciousness. In the same way that the dreamer is experiencing the dream through the point of view of the character, this consciousness is experiencing life through the "me." Needless to say, this is a pull-the-rug from under your feet kind of revelation.

Self-realization is the understanding that we are so much more than the self we take ourselves to be. It has a way of reorganizing our whole approach to life from a narrow self-orientation into a much more expansive one. It's similar to when we wake up in the morning, when everything that seemed so important and critical in the dream has somehow lost its weight. The difference is when we spiritually awaken, we don't stop living that dream. We still have a life and responsibilities along with all our humanity to be with, but now we know things are not exactly what they seem.

This expansive perspective is like the opening of a camera lens where the aperture opens to capture available light. The delineation between the "sense of self" and the rest of life thins out so our well-being is no longer attached to our localized sense of identity. What seemed so relevant in the dream, getting the carrot or outrunning the bag of shit, has far fewer implications.

THE SNOOZE BUTTON

It's not uncommon to have deep spiritual experiences and a profound recognition of the interconnectedness of life, only to slip back into our old, habitual, and limited perspectives. Every time I had an awakening experience, and the veil of my conditioned reality lifted, life became much clearer. I was certain I would never fall back into the old, contracted view. Despite my best efforts to stay awake, however, the "me" would find a way to come back online and want to do something with it—keep it, enjoy it, etc. By the time I tried to sustain this heightened experience, it was already too late because the ego was back in the driver's seat. The self, the protagonist in my dream, had again reintroduced its agenda. It wanted to hold on to this realization as if it were a kind of possession.

The spiritual self still thinks it can find a way around impermanence. When "I" want to see everything, including myself, as one, some form of the ego persists and demands the world be seen in a certain way. People often ask themselves, "How do I get that back? How could I have forgotten? It was so clear just a few moments ago." These thoughts, however, are part of the dynamic that pushes insight and revelation back into the background. The clarity came about in the first place by recognizing all agendas exist within the dream, so the moment we impose our demands on what's happening, we're sleeping again.

But once we see what's possible, the idea of going back to the way life "used to be" is no longer appealing. This is a double-edged sword because it serves the purpose of strengthening the commitment to a true inquiry, but it also activates the drive to get somewhere other than here. This seeking energy will do anything to get back there, and if you are anything like me, you will sit for hours to try and regain it. My teacher used to say, "We knock at the door, but we can't force grace to open." That didn't dissuade me from still trying. All of my seeking served the purpose of keeping me "knocking at the door."

This was the first time in my life that more work didn't translate into more results. It wasn't about knocking more or seeking harder; this was clearly out of my control. Recognizing that we aren't able to will our way into awakening can be a massive blow to the egoic construct of seeking. Stopping can be terrifying, though, particularly for the spiritual persona. To not seek feels completely counter to everything we've been conditioned to do.

The opening that comes from interrupting all strategies, though, particularly the spiritual ones, provides an opportunity for great transformation. It can let the peace that we've been chasing finally catch up to us and become the foundation for a new way of thinking, being, and doing.

For me, this transformation was abrupt and shocking. I had had many powerful spiritual experiences in my life, but this wasn't one of them, because it actually felt devastating. The best way to explain this is through the analogy of a balloon with a pinprick hole in it. For as long as I could remember, I was committed to keeping this balloon (my egoic self) as inflated as possible. But no matter how much air I blew in it, the balloon would always gradually deflate. I had to keep up with blowing air (doing), because a deflated balloon was crushing to whatever identity I was holding dear at the time.

It often felt like my drive was outpacing the deflation, and I felt great, but slowing down was inconceivable. On day six of a nine-day silent retreat, in the middle of an otherwise average meditation, this pinprick hole became a gash. My initial reaction was to try to patch things together, to blow more quickly, but it was now impossible to keep up. There was nowhere for the air to go because the "me" had lost its container. The balloon fizzled and the layer that gave form to all the cherished definitions was no more. It didn't feel like an accomplishment; it felt more like total defeat, a snuffing out of the flame that fueled so much of my behavior.

I was left with a perspective rooted in a much greater context. It's not that I woke up, but rather that I came to a deep recognition that the protagonist, being awake (or not) is also happening *within* the dream. I really got that I am not this character I've been taking myself to be, the awake one or the unconscious one; they're all part of the dream. It's as if our localized sense of "I" unhooks from the body and mind and takes on a broader experience of being.

We essentially become life's "witness," and our relationship to the arising conditions we call the world becomes lighter. Things and experiences continue to happen, but these situations are no longer happening to a *me*. Our cherished identities shift from being labels that define us into simply the roles we play. As a result, we feel that we are no longer at the mercy of events and are less contracted and shackled by what used to "knock us down."

STORYTELLERS

Another way to think about spiritual awakening is as stepping out of the trance of our story. We're all probably familiar with going about our days inattentively; maybe we're driving and all of a sudden realize we've been in our minds, caught in some fantasy with no basis in what was happening in the moment. These may seem like moments when we check out into story land, but how checked in are we during what we call our normal lives?

It takes a lot of openness to accept the idea that everything that's ever happened in our lives only lives in memory. The past is just a story, playing out in our minds like a movie. Stories may seem or appear to be true, but they are limited to the mind's concoction of what it can recall. In reaction, our minds may put forth a convincing counterargument like, "Are you telling me what happened yesterday didn't actually happen? Are you saying I didn't have that conversation with my wife last night?"

Grappling with this concept can be incredibly challenging, but we can use the mind to test the argument's validity. If we are able to slow things down, it's not hard to conclude what did or didn't happen yesterday is just a memory. If, by chance, other people were around, their recollections of what may or may not have happened will undoubtedly differ. We are so used to taking our stories at face value, but they're usually far from being the absolute truth. Despite knowing better, we live our lives pretending our subjective and limited perceptions are complete.

In this moment, anything that is not here *right now* is simply a recollection in the mind. If we look closely enough, however, even what is here now is being perceived through the senses and filtered through our lens of conditioning. What we see is actually in the past, as it takes time for light to travel and be processed through our sight. Our experience of the *now* is not a static snapshot, but rather a continuous flow of images of the past. Any attempt to objectify what is happening is already in our memory.

So, what is actually here independent of our subjective filters? I was once asked, "What do I know to be true with such certainty that I would be willing to bet my loved one's life on?" It stopped me in my tracks because it raised the stakes to such a degree that I had to really sit with the question and be absolutely certain of my answer. Right out of the gate, historical "facts" or even things like my name didn't pass the test, as they were based on memory and dependent on my stories. I just didn't have enough evidence to declare them universal truths. Eventually, however, I got to more existential "truths" as I came up with answers like, "I am," or "This is it," or "I exist." But even those conclusions were based on a past, even if it was an immediate past. My sense of self was a perception, which meant it was already being processed by my senses, and this took time. If these conclusions were in the past, they were subject to my mental reasoning. I knew how easy it was for my thinking mind to justify its ideas and how quickly those could be altered by minor, external interventions, so I was skeptical. My mind's opinions seemed fine for normal occasions, but they were not something I would wager someone's life on. I was stunned and left empty-handed, with nothing but a gaping silence.

From this perspective, nothing is absolutely true. Even time and space, as we normally experience them, are also subjective because they are constructs of our linear mind that do not objectively "exist." The idea that space is a three-dimensional grid encompassing all possible locations and that time is a one-dimensional continuum, with now as the origin from which to gauge duration, past, or future, is based on Newtonian physics. This made sense until Einstein's special theory of relativity, where every moment or particular space-time event is described as a "here-now" or a world point. In this universe, there is no such thing as absolute time.

We may read a mathematical theory like this and find it fascinating; we may even quote it, but to actually assimilate it can be a hard pill to swallow. If linear time, the canvas on which our stories are written, is subjective and relative, then nothing that is scribed on the canvas can be taken as an absolute truth. Stories, by definition, require a memory of the past or projection into the future, so they do, in fact, need that canvas.

The core story at the root of all suffering is our identity as individual beings. Applying this same examination to our individuality has the potential to transform everything. "Who am I if I can't define myself through memories of the past?" Even concluding, "I am this man writing this book," is a collection of images, collected in the past and processed by the conditioning of my mind. If I had a completely different set of conditioned beliefs, I would have a completely different set of responses. In this moment, as you are reading this book, and without referring to your memory, what is true?

When I realized all I had been so invested in believing to be true required the next thought just to exist, I found myself simultaneously relieved and in a state of shock. The story of your life is just that…a story. It's like being fully invested in a movie, but then the house lights come up and you realize it was only a movie. It's not as if the experiences unfolding in life suddenly stop; there is no intermission. Life keeps being life. The question now is how can we relate to the tales of our life more skillfully, when we know they are only stories? At this point, I found it vitally important to stop focusing on how I could keep myself awake and pay close attention to the ways in which I habitually put myself back to sleep.

ULTIMATE FREEDOM

We must learn to reawaken and keep ourselves awake, not by mechanical means, but by an infinite expectation of the dawn.
—HENRY DAVID THOREAU

Wouldn't it be nice if there were actually some kind of finish line in life? The spiritual ego would love to find a place where it could arrive and finally claim harbor with a new awakened identity or enlightened state to uphold and protect, like its ideas of Jesus or Buddha. But even the most life-altering transformations can't escape the nature of impermanence. No matter what experiences we have, we are always left with a constant rediscovery of the moment, fresh and new...all the time.

There's a belief that waking up out of the egoic trance and recognizing the illusion of separation will somehow wipe away our conditioning and ultimately resolve the issues we have adopted along the way. It certainly makes the baggage a lot easier to look at and deal with, because now you're less identified with it, but you will still have to tend to your humanity before, during, and after the awakening.

I wouldn't say "be careful what you wish for," but this awakening has the potential to foundationally uproot your life. That's a good thing, because when we wake up, it's like someone has turned up the brightness and illuminated pretty much everything, even the things we didn't want to see. We are given the opportunity to learn how to live from a completely different orientation. Relationships and dynamics that were once amusing now seem foreign, and behaviors that are inconsistent with our truest expression don't seem to fit. It's not uncommon to develop a desire toward isolation and an impulse to reevaluate everything. Like all other things, this also seems to have to run its course.

JUST SHOW UP

I was baffled when I watched a group of visiting Tibetan monks create intricate sand mandalas on the beach. The monks would go out during low tide and spend hours making the detailed mandala designs, only to have them wash away during high tide. To me, the exercise seemed so humbling, because the following day, there they were, repeating the process all over again. They were doing it for the love of it. They don't battle impermanence and transience but recognize it as the magic of experience.

When we are able to stop ourselves, however briefly, from going back to sleep, impermanence stops being something to work around and instead becomes life's gift. No matter how lost we become in the daydream or how tall the ego has built its castle of sand, an instant of awakening has the capacity to wash it away like the high tide. We can't force or will our way into awakening, but we can play an important role in the process by simply showing up.

Showing up means becoming increasingly aware of all the mental, emotional, physical, and spiritual ways we go back to sleep and reidentify with the mask of "me." It allows us to examine all the stories we hold dear and the identities we tend to cling to: a kind person, a spiritual person, a smart person, a not-so-smart person, etc. I've met many ardent spiritual seekers who are very committed to waking up, but they don't want to let go of certain ideas of who they are. Our identities, both positive and negative, are ways of keeping our egoic sense of self in its place.

Even after profound awakening experiences, I still held on to my identity of being a good parent with a vice grip. I was terrified of what truly "letting go" would mean, because I cherished being viewed or defined as a loving father. My mind was using the love for my kids to justify its attachment to the role. It wasn't until I was willing to surrender this as an identity that I began to tap into a whole new way to parent. I was no longer invested in what my parenting meant about me, so I didn't need to manage how I was being perceived. I got to love like I never had loved before. I had a willingness to mess up and start all over, whenever needed. The more I let go, the more I enjoyed being a loving father. Showing up involves a willingness to give up our stories, especially the ones we hold on to most tightly.

When we are fully here, we become more aware of how we can fall back asleep by plugging back into old patterns and conditioning. Surrendering these stories requires courage and commitment. What I find especially fascinating is how the egoic mind tries to hold on and ask, "Yes, but then what?" The ego never gets tired of justifying and validating its narrative. If I don't hold on to my parenting story, does it mean I will ignore my kids and not take care of them? Of course not! We can play the game while being fully aware that it is just that, a game, and then we can even play more fully.

We love our stories. They can be both terrifying and beautiful. Beautiful or not, they no longer need to form the basis of our reality or the foundation of our existence. They can still serve the purpose of helping us operate in a social context, but we don't have to tell a story to love our children deeply or help a stranger, for that matter.

NO SELF, NO PROBLEM

When the sense of "me" as the center of existence disappears, we recognize ourselves as one with our surroundings. We were the drop of water defending its identity as a separate entity, but we now realize we are the entirety of the ocean. There is a saying in spiritual circles that states, "No self, no problem." At this point, the arising of the ego has ceased to be an issue because it is seen for what it is: a temporary performance of certain, often necessary, functions. The formation of the self becomes like a flower budding, unfolding, and then dying.

The utility of a separate entity is helpful for certain aspects and tasks of the human experience; however, there is no longer a need to identify with a "me" behind this process. We go on living, and while the masks we wear remain, there is no longer a persona, or a separate "real" identity, behind the mask. These are now the masks the universe, rather than I, as an individual, wears. The ego recreating itself becomes a process of putting on different disguises that are simply part of the fun.

COMFY EMPTINESS

One of my teachers, Adyashanti, refers to the process of waking from the dream or stepping out of the story as "simplified duality." The convoluted, sticky world of appearances has been simplified. While before there was you, as the character, along with everyone and everything else, now it has been narrowed down into two components: the dreamer and the dreamed. What was once a dream, becomes a lucid dream. Whereas before we were entirely caught up in and identified with our stories, we are now what witnesses the stories and recognizes them as not inherently real. We are still living life, but with a much greater awareness of the emptiness or insubstantiality of our experiences.

There is still a subtle separation in that framework, though. This separation is different from what we experienced when we were fully asleep. When caught in the dream, we see each thing in the dream as separate and as something happening to us. Now the illusion of me has faded and our perspective as the witness is rooted in a much broader reference point. But there is still a seer, separate from the happenings of the dream. This transcendent outlook is witnessing and relating to everything that happens from a comfortable distance as if it were a spectator and can therefore become indifferent and disengaged.

WAKING UP   •   199

Sometimes this is referred to as being "stuck in emptiness" or "drunk on your own realization." The witness consciousness is such a comfortable place for the ego to reside. It can be like having box seats at a sporting event. You get to watch things from the safety of your spiritual walls without all the "noise" from the crowd. Many people with deep realizations stay there for a very long time, while others never seem to come out of this so-called safety. The remains of the egoic identity love it when we stay safe. Getting to this awakened perspective is where most spiritual teachings are aimed. Few spiritual teachers ever speak of getting out of this spiritual booth and back into the court.

JUMPING BACK IN

To study the self is to forget the self. And to forget the self is to be enlightened by the ten thousand things.
—DŌGEN, Founder of Japanese Sōtō Zen

When this experience of our more transcendent sense of self matures, we begin to lose our fascination with its indifference to the drama of life. In fact, our greater lucidity leads to a new relationship with life that is characterized by greater love and compassion. If our dragons aren't real, our lives become a lot less scary. We can now relate to our fears with love rather than anxiety. We are able to do this because we know they are fabrications or stories of the mind.

This reentering into story land is a counterintuitive step, as it's a movement back into the dream that we were originally transcending out of. The return, however, allows us to meet our shadows, the disenfranchised parts of our experience, with all the love they have been seeking. Imagine waking up in the middle of the nightmare and then going back to experience it, but now armed with the knowing that you are, in fact, the dreamer. The question now becomes, how would you relate to the fears and concerns of the nightmare? Would you ready yourself for battle, run like hell, or just enjoy the adventure?

The freedom we once valued for liberating us from our suffering begins to develop a natural impulse to reengage with our identities in a different way. The perceived distance between the witness consciousness and what it witnesses collapses and the seen and the seer are recognized as inseparable.

We see the stories of our lives as mere fabrications used for reaching all the nooks and crannies that need to be reminded of their wholeness. It's like we are both lucidly dreaming and recognizing that everything appearing within the dream is inseparable from the dreamer. With this awakened stance, we feel the fear of rejection, and we make so much room for it that it feels unconditionally accepted.

We shift from being untouched by life to being deeply moved by it. This "reengaging" can be frightening, because it means going back to what we spent so much energy trying to avoid. It seems irrational that we would give up our coveted freedom and consciously reimmerse ourselves in the limitations of the body, mind, and emotions. Only now, something is different.

CHAPTER 12

THE PARADOX OF BEING

All this exploration ultimately leads us right back to where we started, right here and right now. Except that we are now capable of truly being here. Not because we are special or because we know something; quite the contrary, our not knowing and our ordinariness allow us to meet the moment anew. All that's left is a deep devotion for life as it shows up and a natural impulse to be fully alive. We can act, naturally and spontaneously, from a more comprehensive perspective on who we are and who we are meant to be. We are aware that all that arises, however unpleasant it may be, is finding its way back to itself, whether it knows this or not. Every experience is met in such an intimate manner that it dissolves the perceived boundaries between the self and others, between heaven and earth.

THE HUMAN EXPERIENCE

There is no question that being a human being is a wild adventure. Our bodies age, ache, deteriorate, and we will inevitably experience loss at some point or another along the way. Naturally, there is an instinct to try and escape this and find a way to transcend whatever we might find unpleasant. This pushing and pulling are part of the natural movement of life, which we are not exempt from. Desires and preferences are not something to deny, as many spiritual teachings dictate, but rather key ingredients in the unfoldment of life. Our very existence is a function of this resistance and attachment. It is the polarity that attracts the bee to the flower and what gave birth to all of us.

BEN

An elderly friend of mine, whom we'll call Ben, lost his wife and life partner of over thirty years. As one could expect, Ben found himself very sad. He couldn't stop crying and truly missed being with the love of his life. Even though it had been a few months since her passing, Ben said the hurt was so profound that he didn't know if he could bear it.

I sat and listened. At one point, he stopped and turned toward me. "You know, I knew loving this much was risky. But I would do it all over again, even if it meant hurting like this for the rest of my life." Ben had loved all the way. Early in their relationship, despite his best efforts, life had stripped him of all his safety mechanisms. It had been many years since things were out of his control.

THE PARADOX OF BEING · 203

The human experience is not meant to be a safe journey. It's a wacky ride, and that is what makes it so incredible. Some part of us wants to escape unscratched, and hey, that desire is normal. But deep down, if given the choice, I hope we would choose to risk the heartache that goes along with loving fully over keeping ourselves "safe" with a closed off or guarded heart.

Just because life has its ups and downs doesn't mean we have to be tossed around in the process, though. I once heard someone say, "As long as we think of ourselves as the waves and not the entirety of the ocean, we will always be seasick." Humanity, with all of its hang-ups, is something we can embrace and include in the broader spiritual perspective.

When we recognize we weren't meant to escape this polarity, we stop minding the turbulence of life and no longer look for safety nets along the journey. This "life without nets" approach frees us to live it all, including what our conditioning finds objectionable or uncomfortable, the way my friend Ben loved his wife: fully and completely.

UNLIMITED CONTRADICTIONS

The human mind finds this way of being, the ability to love even what is difficult and unpleasant, as a paradoxical experience. The rational mind can't understand how we are both human, a limited body and intellect, and divine, an unlimited consciousness. The mind approaches "experience" from a dualistic perspective. This duality refers to the separation between self and other, inside and outside,

204 • *THE MYSTERY OF YOU*

between who you believe you are and what you perceive and experience. Non-duality implies oneness, or at least the absence of such separation.

Duality and non-duality are not themselves separate experiences, but a single movement...like two sides of the same coin. What is aware of hearing is not separate from the sound heard or hearing itself. Subject, object, and action as one. The concept of yin and yang in Chinese philosophy describes how apparently opposite forces are actually essential for each other's existence. It embraces duality as integral to non-duality. How can we be one thing and everything simultaneously? How can a wave be both the wave and the ocean?

I once invited my son to draw a tree. He initially sketched the traditional trunk with bushy top. "Can a tree exist without the ground, though?" I asked. After giving his tree a crooked line to stand on, he looked back with a sense of completion. "What about the sun, and the clouds that provide rain, are those not also the tree?" He looked at me for a beat, nodded in recognition and kept drawing. He went on adding more things to his definition of tree while saying, "That's the tree and that's the tree." Eventually he included mountains, birds, there was a house, a stick person, and suddenly he paused, looked at me in shock, and said, "It's all the tree."

This experience is paradoxical when the mind tries to understand it. The mind naturally tries to rationalize things. That is its job, to figure things out. Paradox is a skillful way of easing the mind's concerns when it can't make sense out of an experience. Therein, it becomes a placeholder for the intellectual understanding that will never arrive. As the great twentieth-century physicist Niels Bohr, certainly someone with a supremely rational mind, put it, "The opposite of a correct statement is a false statement. But the opposite of a profound truth may well be another profound truth."

The mind has both great and limited capacities and recognizing its limitations is required to meet the mystery that exists outside of our explanations and stories. What life offers us is a continuous, moment-to-moment invitation to live the unknown from a place of absolute discovery. Such discovery occurs when we replace the impulse to be somewhere else with the ability to live in awe for what is here *right now* and prioritize this way of living above the need for the mind to understand.

BEYOND TWO DIMENSIONS

Wisdom tells me I am nothing. Love tells me I am everything.
And between the two my life flows.
—SRI NISARGADATTA MAHARAJ, Indian spiritual teacher

Scientists continually search for answers to life's biggest and most profound questions. I find it fascinating to watch when they are faced with something they cannot explain. Much of quantum physics resides in the realm of conundrums, paradoxes, and the world of infinite possibilities. While we used to think things could only be expressed as a something, we are now recognizing they are more akin to a field of potential. One of science's great gifts is to take concepts to the boundaries of where the rational mind has to give way to the unknown.

Let's say we are living in a two-dimensional flatland rather than our three-dimensional world, and we perceive life through that two-dimensional lens. Now imagine someone or something drops a three-dimensional sphere that moves in and through our field of perception. In the flatland, this sphere would first appear as a dot, then as a circle, grow and then recede in size, and fade back to a dot as it completes its passage through the perception and experience limited by our two-dimensional world.

Our flatland minds could "understand" a circle as something with a circumference that grows and then diminishes in size. But the flatland mind could not understand or even conceive a three-dimensional sphere passing through our limited perceptual field. If someone told us, as we were stuck in our flatland, what a ball was, we wouldn't be able to understand what they were talking about. Something similar occurs in our three-dimensional world when our mind attempts to understand something beyond our traditional point of reference. That doesn't mean we should simply give up on coming to any kind of understanding, though. It simply means that it serves us well to be open to all the possibilities, even if we can't make sense out of them.

Some of humankind's greatest scientific advances were attempts to comprehend the incomprehensible. Using the language of mathematics, scientists make mysteries somewhat more palatable by turning the ambiguous into probabilities. Some of them have the ability to capture with equations what mystics, philosophers, and artists have long pointed to, like the ephemeral nature of time and space. Spirituality and religion are also ways of approaching this mystery. For centuries, teachers like Buddha, Lao-Tzu, and Jesus Christ have all been trying to communicate a multidimensional, often non-dual experience of reality to our "two-dimensional" minds that operate through separation and distinction. Their teachings frequently employ contradictory methods which point to profound truths whose opposites may also be profound truths.

Our minds have been programmed to understand the world in certain and limited ways, so the jarring teachings of these spiritual paradoxes are, in part, an attempt to trick the mind out of these deep-seated habits. Ultimately, we can appreciate and respond to these invitations by using the mind to bring us to the limits of its capacity so we can take the leap into the realm of the undiscovered.

ALL-INCLUSIVE

This kind of freedom and peace embraces the absolute and the relative, the mundane and the divine. This is the realm where the perceived separation between our sense of self and the rest of existence fades away, leaving a deep intimacy with life as pure, unborn possibility. All existence emerges from this kinetic source and is, at the same time, inseparable from it. This is what I believe is meant by the omnipresence of divinity and what philosophers have been writing about for centuries. World-renowned quantum physicists David Bohm and Basil Hiley refer to it as the "unbroken wholeness of the entire universe" and propose that its fundamental quality is nonlocality.

Now that we're no longer separate from the formerly disenfranchised parts of ourselves and our experience, life becomes an open field of possibilities. A capacity comes online that fuels our courage and lights the way through the darkest corners of our being. As old, conditioned aspects arise, they can be reminded that they, too, are divine. The love they seek has always been within and could never really be bestowed from without. What needed a God is now aware that it *is* God. Unworthiness recognizes what has been missing is the recognition of its essential oneness with all of life, which no amount of external love or validation was ever going to provide.

The love I am referring to is an all-inclusive, redemptive love that isn't based on stories. It's not limited to romantic love or even the care we may feel for a child; it transcends our rational mind. Concepts, including those of freedom and peace, are no longer relevant. This is the energy that moves people to pick up a crying baby or be extraordinarily generous to a total stranger in need. People don't do this because they should. They do it because that is what love does. It is the instinct of life to pick itself up, again and again…

Consciousness has an intuitive regard for itself.
—MEISTER ECKHART, Theologian, Medieval German mystic

THE GIFT OF BEING

As we continue our journey, the wake we leave behind is where the rubber meets the road. The byproduct of what started out as a self-centered quest eventually becomes our greatest offering. We become a beneficial presence in the world simply by living from an open heart and mind. We are compassionate and empathetic, not because we believe we should be or because we can reason ourselves into believing that being compassionate is the right thing to do; we embody these qualities because it is our natural impulse to do so.

Think of it like this: we are walking down the street and we suddenly fall and skin our knee. Without even "thinking" about it, we pick ourselves up and tend to our wounds. We do this without thinking we should show compassion and care for ourselves. We do it for one simple reason, our knee hurts. We don't need to create some kind of story about what happened, remind ourselves that it is the right thing to do, or make sure someone is aware of how kind we were to our knee. We don't need anything to motivate us to take care of our wounded knee. We simply do what needs to be done.

Likewise, when we see and hold ourselves as all of life and recognize "it's all the tree," we don't need stories to motivate us to encounter every moment of experience with that kind of love and care. I hope, very soon, we can look back on some things we take for granted today, such as ignoring and walking past someone in the street who is hurting and asking for help, as unsound. That would be as unthinkable as saying to someone who has fallen, including yourself, "I'm not going to tend to your wound, because if I ignore you, maybe you'll learn not to make the mistake of falling again."

When we bring an open heart to life, our presence becomes a light that invites others to see and recognize that light within themselves. This can happen in business, relationships, parenting, or wherever we may find ourselves. It requires truly meeting the people we encounter in our everyday lives as they are, not as we think they should be. I was a much better father to my son, a much better steward of his learning, and provided him with much clearer direction, when I met his defiance with love rather than judgment about how he "should" or "shouldn't" behave when roughhousing with his sister.

This is not an idealized, perfect version of a human; it's simply one that embraces its humanity as part of the whole. We get to live from a place of openness and recognize a sense of responsibility, as in the "ability to respond," for how we live. The way we now show up in business and relationships, while driving a car, or walking down the street is an expression of our deepest truth. We can't underestimate the influence we have on others; we really can be a redeeming presence everywhere and serve as reminders to ourselves and each other that the wake we leave matters.

○

NOT THE END,
BUT THE BEGINNING

*A human being is a part of the whole called by us universe, a part
limited in time and space. He experiences himself, his thoughts
and feelings as something separated from the rest, a kind of
optical delusion of his consciousness. This delusion is a kind of
prison for us, restricting us to our personal desires and to affection
for a few persons nearest to us. Our task must be to free ourselves
from this prison by widening our circle of compassion to embrace
all living creatures and the whole of nature in its beauty.*
—ALBERT EINSTEIN, Theoretical physicist

We were never taught that suffering was optional. We
were never taught that peace was available even in
the presence of the frailty of the human condition. It's time
for us to update our genetically and culturally inherited

operating system that restricts us to perceiving and experiencing ourselves and the world around us through the lens of separation and scarcity.

This orientation has been in place and running humanity for millennia, even though it has long stopped being effective or even rational. From an early age, we were expected to orient our life from a narrow "me" and "mine" perspective. Our embedded instructions were to protect and defend what enhanced the individual and avoid, at all costs, what we perceived as dangerous or damaging. We learned to survive by having a strong sense of "self" and creating and defending certain identities that defined us. We learned that our well-being was contingent on specific circumstances and therefore attempt to control others as well as our own experience. We innocently subscribed to the notion that we knew what was best.

This programming makes it impossible for us to connect with the more profound and essential realization that there is an intelligence to how everything unfolds, if we would only let it be. One of the best-known expressions of this insight is the Four Noble Truths, which we covered in the beginning.

TRUTH 1: Suffering. Yes, it's true that we do indeed suffer. There's no denying that, as much as we might want or try to.

TRUTH 2: Origin. Our suffering has a cause, which we've been calling the business-as-usual operating system.

TRUTH 3: Cessation. However, suffering will cease if we disrupt and unravel our habitual ways of managing and resisting, rather than experiencing, life.

TRUTH 4: Path. There is a path or means that will lead us out of suffering. The steps along this path can only take place in the moment and from instant to instant. We literally can't postpone freedom or make it dependent on circumstances—on this or that happening first. Since minds have the instinctive habit of saying "then and there" rather than "here and now," the path involves a fundamental shift in how we approach life.

This book is my way of identifying the source of suffering and providing a framework for a way to end it.

At its simplest, suffering arises from resistance. It stems from a closed mind that takes its thoughts and stories as the ultimate truth. These are always based on a past memory, an anticipation of the future, or sometimes both. Therefore, the simplest way to stop suffering is to start where you are. In this very instant you can choose to stop delaying your well-being and become aware of how the mind insists on being somewhere other than in the present moment. This awareness requires that you take full responsibility for how you show up *right now* and makes it easier to notice how to act in harmony with the natural flow of life.

We can always count on life to mirror back whatever is unresolved inside of us. Our deep misunderstandings and psychological wounds will find ways to surface, especially in our relationships. These triggers, however, when approached from a larger context, can be an invitation for us to take responsibility for how we show up and can heal those deep-seated wounds.

By questioning some of our most cherished assumptions, we get to unwind the conditioned habits of resistance that create all the unnecessary stress and anxiety. We have an opportunity to transform our mind as well as our emotional and physical body from centers of conflict into the greatest assets in our journey. Our mind shifts from an overbearing ruler into a tool of creation and our emotions transform from demons to be subdued into welcomed guests that allow us to experience all of life's flavors. We can then stop relating to the body as something that we need to manage and embrace it as a compass or gateway to present-moment experience.

In my mentoring relationships, I have noticed the most successful parents, partners, and businesspeople are those who are able to take full responsibility for their lives. They have both the willingness and humility to reevaluate assumptions and operate with an open heart and mind. This allows them to find the right balance between engagement and surrender in any given situation or challenge by aligning with life's wisdom and showing up as integrated and coherent human beings.

As we know, life is messy, and it's not about our ability to avoid getting our heart broken but the ability to experience love and heartbreak with all of the joys, sorrows, and bliss that go along with it. I have found a peace in the middle of all that imperfection, however, that makes life a much more enjoyable adventure.

Waking up beyond the construct of our limited sense of "me" is the doorway into a completely different experience of being, one where our perspective on life broadens and our troubles are recognized as solely happening in the past or in the future; in other words, their existence is entirely dependent on imagination or memory. This new orientation allows us to operate from an inner calm where we can plan and be totally here. We get to function in time while experiencing timelessness.

Who we are at the core of our being is inseparable from the rest of existence. Enlightenment is not a heightened state of awareness, reserved for the monks and gurus in far-off lands. Enlightenment is something accessible to all of us, even in the midst of our modern-day busy lives. What underlies the entire path is love. Business, parenting, and relationships become the avenues we use to share and embody this love. While the mind may have a conditioned tendency to think that freedom will be experienced and suffering will only end when something changes, the truth is this can only happen in the present moment. Right now. Are you ready? Let's begin.

ABOUT THE AUTHOR

Emilio Diez Barroso was a lifelong seeker—seeking recognition, achievement, love, success, and finally, the ultimate carrot: enlightenment. In his pursuit of enlightenment, he was forced to face the one thing he was desperately trying to avoid: his own sense of unworthiness. Defeated at the game of avoiding and humbled by the realization of his true nature, he is now dedicated to alleviating suffering in the world. Emilio is married and is a father to three incredible teachers. He is an active investor, philanthropist, and entrepreneur and sits on the board of over a dozen for-profit and nonprofit companies. He has a master's in spiritual psychology and resides in Los Angeles, California.

Printed in Great Britain
by Amazon

39699876R00128